Someone's in the Kitchen with

DAYTON'S

Marshall Field's

HUDSON'S

Someone's in the Kitchen with DAYTON'S *Marshall Field's* HUDSON'S

CB
CONTEMPORARY BOOKS
CHICAGO

Acknowledgments

Thanks to all of our food service employees, both past and present, for their hard work and dedication throughout the years. Thanks also to all those who contributed their valuable ideas, creativity, and time to this book.

Many thanks to Jennifer Panchenko for her tireless support of this special project.

Design by Georgene Sainati
Photography by Miles Lowry
Photo assistance by Mel Hill, Ned Bushnell
Foodstyling by Lynn Gagné
Foodstyling assistance by Carol Laureys
Prop styling by Wendy Marx
Prop styling assistance by Kate Qualiardi

Published by Contemporary Books, Inc.
180 North Michigan Avenue, Chicago, Illinois 60601
Manufactured in the United States of America
International Standard Book Number: 0-8092-3822-5

Contents

Introduction.......vii

Soups.......1

Salads.......23

Main-Dish Salads.......47

Main Dishes.......84

Side Dishes.......129

Breads and Muffins.......147

Desserts.......167

Index.......207

Introduction

Dayton's, Marshall Field's, and Hudson's, our family of stores, share a common tradition of delicious foods, freshly prepared and pleasingly served. We're proud that over the years our kitchens, bakeries, and restaurants have become a part of your family's traditions, be it for holiday tea in Marshall Field's Walnut Room, hearthside luncheons at Dayton's Oak Grill, midday excursions to one of our bustling Marketplace delis, or those delicious detours to Hudson's Terrace restaurant.

You've let us know that variety truly is the spice of life when it comes to good food. Since the opening of our very first tearoom in 1890 right up to today—in 1990 Director of Food Services John Lovelace was honored with the prestigious Ivy Award for his creative food concepts—we've enjoyed serving your favorite classics as well as fresh new interpretations of specialty cuisines and light, wholesome meals for people on the go. As for dessert . . . well, our passion for confectionery is no secret! Dayton's mouth-watering chocolates have been part of holiday festivities since 1902 (when George Draper Dayton personally distributed gifts of handmade candies to all store employees), while Marshall Field's has been fashioning its world-famous Frango chocolates since 1929. Today, ours are the only department stores operating two candy kitchens, and we still believe that fine candymaking is an art that can only be done by hand.

Hudson's

Good food and family celebrations have gone hand in hand at

our stores for generations. Since 1925, for instance, Hudson's annual Santa Claus parade through the streets of Detroit has been the colorful prelude to Thanksgiving dinner, while our Freedom Festival, first organized in 1959, is the dazzling setting for summer picnics and the city's most famous fireworks extravaganza. Marshall Field's legendary holiday windows along Chicago's bustling State Street still enchant youngsters of all ages, and the magic of the season wouldn't be quite complete without joining in to watch the lighting of the Great Tree, which stands nearly four stories tall and is adorned with some five thousand handcrafted ornaments, the centerpiece of the Walnut Room. In Minnesota, childhood memories have been made at Dayton's lively Christmas auditorium show since 1963, and that was the same year we held our first Flower Show, such a breathtaking display of blossoms and greenery that friends now come to visit from all over the country each year. Our newest Twin Cities community event is A Cause for Applause, a gala fashion and entertainment festival that benefits children's cancer research.

Marshall Field's

Dayton's

Good times are for sharing, and in that spirit we've collected more than 150 of the best-loved recipes from Dayton's, Marshall Field's, and Hudson's. Now you can prepare such treasured dishes at home as our hearty Boundary Waters Wild Rice Soup (page 12), the perfect start to a winter's meal, or savory Chicken Pie (page 102), which has remained one of our most requested selections since the turn of the century.

For special occasions with family and friends, you'll find elegant soups, salads, entrees, and accompaniments, from our Timbercrest Pasta (page 37) to Fettuccine with Smoked Salmon and Caviar (page 89), plus a delectable array of unforgettable dessert finales including Lemon Soufflé (page 168) and Frango Triple-Treat Chocolate Layer Cake (page 176). From our popular Marketplace Lites come tempting quick-to-fix seasonal soups, fresh salads, and gourmet sandwich creations, all low in fat, calories, and cholesterol.

You've let us be a part of your family gatherings and special meals on so many occasions in so many places. Now we hope you'll enjoy creating the foods you've come to love at Dayton's, Marshall Field's, and Hudson's and treat our cookbook as your recipe box for favorite suppers, memorable meals for guests, delicious healthy options, and sweet new ways to splurge. It's a gift—and a thank-you—from our kitchens to yours. And, of course, it comes with our standing invitation to stop by anytime to sample what our chefs, bakers, and confectioners are cooking up today in the kitchens of Dayton's, Marshall Field's, and Hudson's.

Bon Appétit!

Julie Griffin

Julie Griffin
Senior Buyer Food Division
Cookbook Editor

Soups

Chilled Strawberry Soup *(D)*

Cantaloupe Soup *(D)*

Peach-Plum-Cranberry Soup *(D)*

Vichyssoise *(H)*

Gazpacho *(D, MF, H)*

Zesty Tomato Soup *(D)*

Tortilla Soup *(MF)*

Black Bean Soup *(D)*

Spanish National Soup *(D)*

Manhattan Clam Chowder *(D)*

Boundary Waters Wild Rice Soup *(D)*

Cream of Asparagus Soup *(MF)*

Cream of Fresh Mushroom Soup *(MF)*

Cream of Zucchini and Almond Soup *(MF)*

Roasted Acorn Squash Soup *(D, MF, H)*

Cream of Spinach Soup with Bacon *(D)*

New England Clam Chowder *(MF)*

Lobster Bisque *(H)*

Chicken and Cheese Soup *(D)*

Canadian Cheese Soup *(MF)*

D = Dayton's, *MF* = Marshall Field's, *H* = Hudson's,
MP = Marketplace, *ML* = Marketplace Lites

New England Clam Chowder (page 18), Chicken and Cheese Soup (page 20), and Boundary Waters Wild Rice Soup (page 12)

Chilled Strawberry Soup

In a food processor or blender, puree strawberries with sugar and honey. Add 1 cup of the cream and blend until smooth. Transfer to a large bowl and add remaining cream and the sherry. Chill thoroughly.

1½ pints ripe strawberries, hulled
¼ cup sugar
2 tablespoons honey
4 cups whipping cream
2 tablespoons dry or cream sherry

Makes 6 1-cup servings

Cantaloupe Soup

Peel and seed the cantaloupe and cut into chunks. Puree in a food processor or blender with the honey and sugar. Transfer to a large bowl and mix in the apple juice, lemon juice, liqueur or sherry, and salt. Chill well.

At serving time, whip the cream until it holds soft peaks. Fold into juice mixture. Garnish with strawberry slices.

Makes 6 to 7 1-cup servings

1 medium-size ripe cantaloupe
¼ cup honey
2 tablespoons sugar
1½ cups apple juice
2 tablespoons fresh lemon juice
1–2 tablespoons Midori liqueur or dry sherry
Pinch salt
1½ cups whipping cream
Sliced strawberries for garnish

Peach-Plum-Cranberry Soup

5 cups cranberry juice cocktail
½ cup plus 2 tablespoons sugar
3¾ tablespoons cornstarch
1¼ teaspoons cinnamon
⅛ teaspoon ground cloves
5 ripe peaches or nectarines, peeled, pitted, and sliced thin
5 ripe plums, peeled, pitted, and sliced thin
1 lemon, sliced thin

Combine half the cranberry juice, the sugar, cornstarch, cinnamon, and cloves in a large nonaluminum saucepan, stirring until smooth. Add the remaining cranberry juice.

Heat to a boil over high heat, then cook and stir 1 minute. Reduce heat and add all fruits. Cover and simmer gently 8 to 20 minutes, depending on how ripe fruit is, until it is just tender.

Transfer to a covered container and chill thoroughly before serving.

Makes 8 1-cup servings

Vichyssoise

Slit the leek lengthwise and clean it under cold water. Trim away coarse green top and slice white part into thin slices.

Melt butter in a large saucepan. Add leek, onion, and garlic. Cook gently, stirring often, 8 to 10 minutes until tender. Do not brown.

Add 3 cups of the broth, potatoes, marjoram, paprika, and mace. Cover and simmer gently 30 to 40 minutes until potatoes are very soft.

Strain soup and chill thoroughly. At serving time, stir in cream and add salt and pepper.

If soup is too thick, add additional broth as necessary.

1 large leek
2 tablespoons butter
1 small yellow onion, diced
1 small clove garlic, minced
3 to 4 cups chicken broth
2 large Idaho potatoes, peeled and sliced
¼ teaspoon dried marjoram
Pinch paprika
Pinch mace
3 cups whipping cream
Salt and pepper to taste

Makes 7 1-cup servings

Gazpacho

Mix all ingredients in a large bowl. Chill well before serving.

Makes 10 1-cup servings

- 6½ cups tomato juice
- 1 clove garlic, pressed
- 1 cucumber, seeded and diced fine
- 3 tomatoes, seeded and diced fine
- 4 ounces (1½ cups) sliced mushrooms
- 1 green bell pepper, diced fine
- 1 jar (5 ounces) pimientos, drained and chopped
- 1 medium yellow onion, diced fine
- Juice of 3 lemons
- 2 tablespoons vegetable oil
- 1½ tablespoons sugar
- 1½ teaspoons red wine vinegar
- ½ teaspoon salt
- ⅛ teaspoon pepper
- 4 dashes hot pepper sauce
- 3 dashes Worcestershire sauce

Zesty Tomato Soup

In a medium saucepan, fry bacon until crisp. Drain bacon on paper towels. Spill off all but 2 teaspoons fat.

Add onion to bacon fat and cook over medium heat until tender. Add tomato soup, milk, drained tomatoes, and seasonings. Heat to a simmer. Remove bay leaf.

Crumble bacon and add to soup. Adjust seasoning. Serve hot.

Makes 4 1-cup servings

3 strips bacon
½ small yellow onion, diced
1 10¾-ounce can tomato soup
1 soup can whole milk
1 16-ounce can diced tomatoes, drained
1 bay leaf
1 teaspoon dried thyme
½ teaspoon dried basil
⅛ teaspoon dried oregano
Black pepper to taste

Tortilla Soup

3 corn tortillas
8¾ cups chicken broth
2 tablespoons chopped cilantro
¼ cup vegetable oil
1 medium yellow onion, diced
2 teaspoons cumin
¾ teaspoon turmeric
1 10-ounce box frozen corn
1 jalapeño, seeded and chopped
1 small red bell pepper, diced
1 small green bell pepper, diced
Salt and pepper to taste

Tear tortillas into pieces. Place in a large saucepan with ¾ cup chicken broth. Heat to a boil, cover, and cook gently about 10 minutes until tortillas are mushy. Transfer tortillas and broth to a blender or food processor and add cilantro; blend until smooth. Set aside.

In the same pan, heat oil. Add onion, cumin, and turmeric. Cook gently about 10 minutes until onion is tender. Add remaining broth, corn, and jalapeño. Heat to a boil. Add red and green pepper and pureed tortilla mixture. Cook 15 minutes until peppers are tender.

Add salt and pepper. Serve hot.

Makes 10 1-cup servings

Black Bean Soup

Put beans in a large pot and cover with water. Soak 12 hours or overnight. Drain well and remove from pot.

In same pot, brown salt pork. Add onion, carrot, and celery and cook 5 minutes until they begin to soften.

Add beans, mix well, then add broth and ham. Heat to a boil. Reduce heat and simmer, covered, 2 to 3 hours until beans are tender.

Add salt and pepper to taste. Serve hot, garnished with lemon or chopped egg.

Note: If you want a thicker soup, remove about 2 cups of the cooked beans with a slotted spoon and puree in a blender or food processor; stir puree back into soup.

1 pound dried black beans
2 ounces salt pork, chopped fine
1 medium yellow onion, chopped
2 medium carrots, chopped fine
2 small stalks celery, chopped fine
12 cups chicken broth
⅔ pound ham, diced
Salt and pepper to taste
Thinly sliced lemon or chopped hard-cooked egg for garnish

Makes 10 1-cup servings

Spanish National Soup

Melt the butter or heat the oil in a large saucepan. Add the carrot, celery, and onion. Cook over medium heat, stirring often, 8 to 10 minutes until they begin to soften. Add the chicken broth, salami, ham, chicken, tomatoes, bay leaf, garlic powder, salt, and pepper.

Heat to a boil. Reduce heat and simmer, covered, about 20 minutes until carrot is tender. Add the beans, rice, and parsley. Cook 5 minutes longer. Serve hot.

Makes 8 1-cup servings

2 tablespoons butter or olive oil
½ cup diced carrot
½ cup diced celery
½ cup diced yellow onion
5 cups chicken broth
⅔ cup diced hard salami
⅔ cup diced ham
⅔ cup diced cooked chicken meat
1 16-ounce can diced tomatoes, drained
1 bay leaf
¼ teaspoon garlic powder
Salt and pepper to taste
1 16-ounce can garbanzo beans, drained
1 cup cooked rice
⅓ cup chopped fresh parsley

Manhattan Clam Chowder

Brown the bacon in a large saucepan. Add the potato, onion, celery, green pepper, carrot, and garlic. Cook over medium heat, stirring often, 6 to 8 minutes until the vegetables begin to soften.

Add the crushed tomatoes, clam juice, clams, lobster base, and seasonings. Heat to a boil. Reduce heat and simmer gently, partially covered, about 15 minutes until potato is tender.

Serve hot.

Makes 8 1-cup servings

4 strips bacon, diced
1 cup unpeeled diced Idaho potato
½ cup diced yellow onion
½ cup diced celery
½ cup diced green bell pepper
½ cup diced carrot
1 clove garlic, minced
1 28-ounce can crushed tomatoes
2 8-ounce bottles clam juice
2 6-ounce cans minced clams, drained
2 teaspoons lobster base, optional
½ teaspoon dried thyme
½ teaspoon dried oregano
Salt and pepper to taste

Boundary Waters Wild Rice Soup

6 tablespoons butter
1 small yellow onion, chopped
½ cup all-purpose flour
4 cups chicken broth
1 cup whipping cream
⅓ cup dry sherry
1½ cups cooked wild rice
½ teaspoon white pepper
Salt to taste

Melt butter in a medium pan. Add onion and cook 5 minutes until soft.

Stir in flour and cook 1 minute, stirring often. Add broth and whisk until smooth. Add cream and sherry and heat to a simmer. Add rice, pepper, and salt. Simmer gently 5 minutes, just until heated through and slightly thickened.

Serve hot.

Makes 6 1-cup servings

Cream of Asparagus Soup

Trim the woody ends from the asparagus and peel the stems with a vegetable peeler. Cut the asparagus into 1-inch pieces. Combine in a medium saucepan with onion, chicken broth, and bay leaf. Cover and heat to a boil. Simmer gently 20 to 25 minutes until asparagus is completely soft. Discard bay leaf and puree mixture in a food processor or blender.

1 pound asparagus
1 small yellow onion, chopped
1½ cups chicken broth
1 bay leaf
2 tablespoons butter
2 tablespoons all-purpose flour
2 cups whole milk
½ cup whipping cream
Salt and pepper to taste

In the same pan, melt the butter. Stir in the flour and cook, stirring often, for 1 minute. Whisk in the milk and cream and heat to a simmer. Add the asparagus puree, salt, and pepper. Cook just until heated through.

Serve hot or chilled.

Makes 6 1-cup servings

Cream of Fresh Mushroom Soup

Melt butter and chicken fat in a medium saucepan. Add mushrooms and onion and cook 8 to 10 minutes until tender.

Sprinkle flour in and mix well. Cook 1 minute, stirring constantly. Whisk in milk and chicken broth. Heat just to a simmer and cook gently 6 to 8 minutes until soup thickens slightly.

Add half-and-half and salt. Serve with a drizzle of whipping cream on top.

3 tablespoons butter
3 tablespoons chicken fat (or use 6 tablespoons butter)
4 cups (⅔ pound) finely chopped mushrooms
¼ cup chopped yellow onion
6 tablespoons flour
3 cups whole milk
1 cup chicken broth
⅔ cup half-and-half
Salt to taste
¼ cup whipping cream for serving, if desired

Makes 6 1-cup servings

Cream of Zucchini and Almond Soup

Melt butter in a medium saucepan. Add onion and cook about 5 minutes until tender.

Stir in flour and cook 1 minute. Add broth, zucchini, and slivered almonds. Heat to a boil. Reduce heat and simmer gently, uncovered, about 10 minutes until zucchini is tender.

Add ground almonds, sugar, and seasonings. Simmer 5 minutes longer. Add cream and heat through. Serve hot.

Makes 6 1-cup servings

3 tablespoons butter
⅓ cup minced yellow onion
¼ cup all-purpose flour
5 cups chicken broth
1 large zucchini, sliced
2 tablespoons slivered blanched almonds
2½ tablespoons ground blanched almonds
1 teaspoon light brown sugar
⅛ teaspoon cinnamon
⅛ teaspoon nutmeg
Salt and pepper to taste
⅔ cup whipping cream

Roasted Acorn Squash Soup

1 acorn squash
Salt to taste
2 tablespoons butter
¼ cup chopped celery
¼ cup chopped carrot
2 tablespoons chopped yellow onion
2 cups chicken broth
¼ cup whipping cream
1½ teaspoons fresh lemon juice
Pepper to taste

Preheat oven to 300°F.

Cut squash in half and scrape out seeds and spongy membrane. Rinse seeds and pat dry. Place squash on a jelly roll pan, cut side down. Arrange seeds on a baking sheet.

Bake squash about 1 hour and 15 minutes until completely soft. Bake seeds 25 to 35 minutes until they are crisp and golden. Sprinkle seeds with salt.

In a medium saucepan, melt butter. Add celery, carrot, and onion. Cook gently about 5 minutes until soft.

Scrape flesh from squash and add to pan along with broth. Heat to a boil. Reduce heat, cover, and simmer gently 25 to 30 minutes until the carrot and celery are tender.

Puree soup in a food processor or blender. Return to pan and add cream, lemon juice, salt, and pepper. Gently heat.

Serve soup sprinkled with toasted squash seeds.

Makes 6 1-cup servings

Cream of Spinach Soup with Bacon

2 slices bacon, diced fine
2 tablespoons finely chopped yellow onion
½ cup (1 stick) butter
½ cup all-purpose flour
3½ cups chicken broth
3½ cups whole milk
2 tablespoons dry white wine
1 10-ounce box frozen whole leaf spinach, thawed
Seasoned salt to taste
Freshly ground white pepper to taste

In a large saucepan, fry the bacon until crisp. Shortly before it is finished, stir in the onion and cook until soft. Add the butter. When the butter is melted, stir in the flour. Cook, stirring often, for 1 minute.

Whisk in the chicken broth, then add the milk and wine.

Squeeze the excess water from the spinach and chop the spinach coarsely. Add it to the soup. Heat to a simmer, then cook gently 5 minutes. Add seasoned salt and pepper.

Serve hot.

Makes 8 1-cup servings

New England Clam Chowder

1 cup peeled, diced potato
4 tablespoons butter
½ cup chopped celery
½ cup chopped yellow onion
⅔ cup all-purpose flour
4 cups whole milk
Salt and pepper to taste
1 cup chopped clams
1 cup clam juice

Cook potato in boiling water about 10 minutes until it is tender but not mushy. Drain well and set aside.

Melt the butter in a medium saucepan. Add celery and onion and cook 5 to 6 minutes until soft. Stir in flour and cook 1 minute.

Add milk, salt, and pepper. Heat gently to a simmer. Cook, uncovered, 15 minutes.

Add potato, clams, and clam juice and simmer 5 minutes longer. Serve hot.

Makes 8 1-cup servings

Lobster Bisque

Melt butter in a medium pan. Stir in flour and cook 1 minute. Add water, whisking until smooth. Add lobster base and cayenne pepper. Heat to a boil.

Add half-and-half, sherry, and lobster. Cook gently just until heated through. Serve hot.

Makes 8 1-cup servings

½ cup (1 stick) butter
¾ cup all-purpose flour
5½ cups water
3 tablespoons lobster base
Dash cayenne pepper
2 cups half-and-half
6 tablespoons dry sherry
6 ounces canned lobster meat, including liquid

Chicken and Cheese Soup

Melt the butter in a large saucepan. Add the carrot, celery, and onion. Cook over medium heat, stirring often, about 8 minutes until the onion is tender.

½ cup (1 stick) butter
¼ cup diced carrot
¼ cup diced celery
¼ cup diced yellow onion
½ cup all-purpose flour
3 cups whole milk
2 cups chicken broth
¾ cup diced cooked chicken
1 11-ounce can cheddar cheese soup
¼ cup (1 ounce) shredded cheddar cheese
1 tablespoon dry white wine or dry vermouth
⅛ teaspoon garlic salt
Salt and pepper to taste

Sprinkle the flour over and mix in. Add the milk and chicken broth, whisking until smooth. Heat to a simmer and cook gently, uncovered, about 10 minutes until the carrot is tender.

Add the chicken, cheese soup, cheese, wine or vermouth, garlic salt, salt, and pepper, whisking thoroughly. Heat through.

Serve hot.

Makes 7 1-cup servings

Canadian Cheese Soup

Melt butter in a large saucepan. Add onion, celery, and carrot. Cook gently, stirring often, about 10 minutes until vegetables begin to soften.

In a small dish, mix flour, cornstarch, paprika, and baking soda. Add to vegetables and cook, stirring constantly, 1 minute.

Add milk and broth, whisking until smooth. Heat to a simmer. Cover and cook gently, stirring often, about 10 minutes until carrot is tender.

Remove pan from heat. Add cheese and stir until smooth. Add bitters.

Add salt and pepper to taste. Serve hot with a sprinkling of parsley.

4 tablespoons butter
1 tablespoon finely chopped yellow onion
½ cup very finely diced celery, cooked
½ cup very finely diced carrot, cooked
½ cup all-purpose flour
1 tablespoon cornstarch
⅛ teaspoon paprika
⅛ teaspoon baking soda
3 cups whole milk
3 cups chicken broth
2 pounds aged sharp cheddar cheese, shredded
2 drops bitters
Salt and pepper to taste
Minced parsley for garnish

Makes 8 1-cup servings

Salads

Fruit Ambrosia Salad *(H)*

Tropical Breeze Salad *(ML)*

Waldorf Salad *(H)*

Tropical Layered Salad *(ML)*

Carrot, Raisin, and Nut Salad *(MF)*

Boiled Dressing *(MF)*

New Potato Salad *(ML)*

German Potato Salad *(H)*

Peanut Cole Slaw *(MF)*

Seafood Slaw *(H)*

Kidney Bean Salad *(H)*

Mixed Bean Salad *(MF)*

Gremolata Bean Salad *(ML)*

Timbercrest Pasta *(MP)*

Black-Eyed Pea Salad *(ML)*

Country Fresh Salad *(MP)*

Spinach Rice Salad *(MP)*

Traditional Greek Salad *(D)*

Pasta Primavera *(MP)*

Lemon Pasta Salad with Basil, Tomato, and Parmesan *(MP)*

Pesto Pasta *(ML)*

Greek Pasta and Feta Salad *(MP)*

D = Dayton's, *MF* = Marshall Field's, *H* = Hudson's,
MP = Marketplace, *ML* = Marketplace Lites

◀ *Citrus Turkey Salad (page 71)*

Fruit Ambrosia Salad

1 16-ounce can cling peach halves
1 16-ounce can pear halves
1 16-ounce can pineapple tidbits
1 14-ounce can mandarin orange sections
2 cups (8 ounces) chopped walnuts
1⅔ cups flaked coconut
1½ cups whipping cream or 3 cups frozen whipped dessert topping

Place all fruits in a large colander placed over a bowl. Allow to drain overnight in the refrigerator.

Cut the peaches and pears into cubes. Combine all the fruits, walnuts, and coconut in a large bowl.

If you are using whipping cream, whip it until it holds soft peaks. Fold the whipped cream or whipped topping into the fruit mixture.

Serve well chilled.

Makes 8 to 10 servings

Tropical Breeze Salad

Peel and core pineapple. Cut into bite-sized chunks. Peel and seed papaya. Cut into bite-sized chunks. Peel kiwifruit and cut into eight slices. Place pineapple, papaya, kiwifruit, strawberries, and banana in a serving bowl.

In a separate bowl, combine dressing ingredients. Pour over fruit and mix well. Top with almonds.

Serve chilled.

Makes 8 to 10 servings

SALAD

½ pineapple
1½ papayas
1 kiwifruit
1½ cups halved strawberries
1½ bananas, sliced

DRESSING

¼ cup plain low-fat yogurt
1 teaspoon honey
1½ teaspoons frozen orange juice concentrate
½ tablespoon poppy seeds
Pinch freshly grated lemon peel
Pinch freshly grated orange peel

2 tablespoons sliced toasted almonds

Waldorf Salad

4 cups unpeeled diced red-skinned apples
3 tablespoons fresh lemon juice
1½ cups diced celery
¾ cup chopped walnuts
1 cup frozen whipped dessert topping
⅓ cup mayonnaise
Sugar and/or salt to taste

Place apples in a large bowl and toss with lemon juice. Add celery and walnuts and mix well.

Add whipped topping, mayonnaise, and sugar and salt as desired.

Chill well before serving.

Makes 6 to 8 servings

Tropical Layered Salad

In a blender, puree yogurt, cottage cheese, 1 banana, and lemon juice.

Place spinach on a serving plate. Slice the remaining bananas. Arrange bananas, pineapple, orange, and papaya on top of spinach. Top with yogurt mixture and garnish with toasted coconut.

Serve chilled.

Makes 8 to 10 servings

¼ cup plain low-fat yogurt
½ cup cottage cheese
3 bananas
2 teaspoons lemon juice
¼ pound fresh spinach, stemmed and washed
2 cups fresh pineapple chunks
2 oranges, peeled and sectioned
1 papaya, peeled and cubed
2 tablespoons toasted coconut

Carrot, Raisin, and Nut Salad

Combine Boiled Dressing and mayonnaise in a medium bowl.

Add carrots, raisins, and nuts and toss to combine.

Chill well before serving.

Makes 5 1-cup servings

⅓ cup Boiled Dressing (see page 29 for recipe)
⅓ cup mayonnaise
1 pound carrots, peeled and shredded
1 cup raisins
⅓ cup chopped walnuts or pecans

Boiled Dressing

Place sugar, mustard, salt, and flour in a heatproof bowl and mix together. Add egg and blend well. Set aside.

In a saucepan, combine vinegar and water. Heat until mixture comes to a boil. Pour into egg mixture and beat well.

Place mixture in the saucepan. Over medium heat, cook until mixture thickens, stirring constantly to prevent scorching. Add butter or margarine and stir until melted. Remove from heat.

Chill in a covered container before using.

2 tablespoons sugar
1 teaspoon dry mustard
½ teaspoon salt
2 tablespoons all-purpose flour
1 egg
½ cup cider vinegar
½ cup water
1 tablespoon butter or margarine

Makes about 1¼ cups

New Potato Salad

Cut potatoes into quarters and boil about 15 minutes until soft. Chill. Place potatoes, green onion, celery, and egg in a serving bowl.

Blend together mayonnaise, mustard, and vinegar. In a small bowl, mix together celery seed, sugar, salt, and pepper. Add to mayonnaise mixture and blend well. Pour over potatoes and mix well.

Serve chilled.

SALAD

2½ pounds tiny red new potatoes
¼ cup sliced green onion
¾ cup chopped celery
2 eggs, hard-cooked, peeled, and sliced

DRESSING

¾ cup mayonnaise
2 teaspoons Dijon mustard
2 teaspoons red wine vinegar
1½ teaspoons celery seed
1 teaspoon sugar
1 teaspoon salt
1 teaspoon pepper

Makes 8 to 10 servings

German Potato Salad

Cook potatoes in boiling water 12 to 25 minutes until they can easily be pierced with the tip of a sharp knife. Drain. Cube potatoes when they are cool enough to handle.

2 pounds small red potatoes
¼ pound bacon
Vegetable oil
½ small yellow onion, diced
⅓ cup white or cider vinegar
Salt and pepper to taste

Cook bacon in a skillet until crisp. Remove to a paper towel to drain. Crumble when it is cool enough to handle.

Pour bacon fat into a measuring cup. If necessary, add vegetable oil to measure ⅓ cup. Return fat mixture to skillet. Add onion and cook, stirring often, about 5 minutes until soft.

Add vinegar, potatoes, bacon, salt, and pepper and toss to combine. Serve warm.

Makes 6 servings

Peanut Cole Slaw

½ cup Boiled Dressing (see page 29 for recipe)
½ cup mayonnaise
1 tablespoon sugar
1 tablespoon cider vinegar
½ teaspoon pepper
4 cups shredded cabbage
½ cup salted dry-roasted peanuts, chopped
2 tablespoons chopped green bell pepper
2 tablespoons chopped pimiento
1 tablespoon chopped yellow onion

Combine Boiled Dressing, mayonnaise, sugar, vinegar, and pepper in a mixing bowl. Mix together well.

Add remaining ingredients and toss to combine.

Chill well before serving.

Makes 8 ½-cup servings

Seafood Slaw

Slice cabbages into ¼-inch strips. In a serving bowl, mix together cabbages, shrimp, seafood flakes, green pepper, and onion.

In a separate bowl, combine mayonnaise and sugar. Add to cabbage mixture and mix well.

Serve chilled.

Makes 8 to 10 servings

1 pound green cabbage
1 pound red cabbage
1 pound cooked salad shrimp
⅔ pound seafood flakes
⅔ green bell pepper, julienned
¼ red onion, julienned
1 cup mayonnaise
1¼ teaspoons sugar

Kidney Bean Salad

Combine all ingredients in a medium bowl. Chill well before serving.

Makes 6 to 8 servings

2 16-ounce cans kidney beans, drained
¼ cup slivered yellow onion
¼ cup chopped celery
2 tablespoons chopped dill pickle
2 tablespoons chopped green bell pepper
⅓ cup mayonnaise
Salt and pepper to taste

Mixed Bean Salad

Drain kidney beans and garbanzo beans. Rinse well and drain thoroughly. Transfer to a large bowl and add green beans, wax beans, lima beans, onion, celery, and green pepper.

1 16-ounce can kidney beans
1 16-ounce can garbanzo beans
1 16-ounce can cut green beans, drained
1 16-ounce can cut wax beans, drained
1 10-ounce box frozen lima beans, thawed
¼ cup chopped yellow onion
¼ cup chopped celery
3 tablespoons chopped green bell pepper
¾ cup white vinegar
½ cup sugar
¾ teaspoon celery seed
¾ teaspoon mustard seeds
½ teaspoon salt

Combine vinegar, sugar, celery seed, mustard seeds, and salt in a small pan. Heat to a boil, stirring to dissolve sugar.

Cool slightly, then pour over salad and toss well. Chill well before serving.

Makes 12 to 16 servings

Gremolata Bean Salad

Soak beans overnight. Drain and rinse beans and place in a large pot. Cover with water and boil 1 to 1½ hours until tender, adding water if needed to keep beans covered.

⅔ pound black beans, dry
¼ lemon, grated rind and juice
½ tablespoon minced garlic
⅓ cup red wine vinegar
4 tablespoons extra-virgin olive oil
1 tablespoon fresh lemon juice
½ tablespoon salt
½ tablespoon black pepper
1 red bell pepper, chopped fine
2–3 celery ribs, chopped fine
1 cup chopped red onion
¾ cup finely chopped cilantro

In a serving bowl, mix together lemon rind and juice, garlic, vinegar, olive oil, lemon juice, salt, and pepper. Add red pepper, celery, onion, and cilantro and mix. Chill.

Drain, rinse, and chill cooked beans. Combine with vegetable and dressing mixture and mix well.

Makes 8 to 10 servings

Timbercrest Pasta

- 1 pound extra-wide egg noodles
- 3 cups broccoli flowerets
- 1 14-ounce can artichoke hearts, drained and quartered
- 1½ cups sliced black olives
- 6 ounces (2¼ cups) sliced mushrooms
- 1 cup slivered sun-dried tomatoes (see Note)
- 1 bunch green onions, cut into rings
- 2¼ cups prepared Italian dressing
- 1 tablespoon dried basil
- ¾ teaspoon garlic salt
- ¾ teaspoon pepper

Cook pasta according to directions on package. About 1 minute before pasta is finished, add broccoli. Drain in a colander and rinse under cold water to stop the cooking. Drain well, shaking colander to remove as much water as possible.

Transfer pasta and broccoli to a large bowl. Add artichoke hearts, olives, mushrooms, sun-dried tomatoes, and green onion. Mix well.

Toss with dressing, basil, garlic salt, and pepper. Chill well before serving.

Note: Oil-packed sun-dried tomatoes may be patted dry and used as is. If you are using dry-pack tomatoes, steam them for 5 minutes to soften before using.

Makes 6 to 8 servings

Black-Eyed Pea Salad

- 2 cups cooked black-eyed peas
- 4 cups cooked white rice
- 1 cup chopped yellow onion
- ½ cup finely chopped celery
- ½ cup chopped red bell pepper
- ½ cup white wine vinegar
- 3 tablespoons extra-virgin olive oil
- 1 teaspoon coarsely ground black pepper
- 1 clove garlic, minced
- Dash hot pepper sauce to taste

In a serving bowl, combine black-eyed peas, rice, onion, celery, and red pepper.

In a small bowl, mix together vinegar, olive oil, pepper, garlic, and hot pepper sauce. Add to black-eyed pea mixture and toss well.

Chill for at least three hours, if possible, to allow flavors to blend.

Makes 8 to 10 servings

Country Fresh Salad

In a serving bowl, combine broccoli, onion, cheese, and bacon.

In a separate bowl, mix together mayonnaise, sugar, and vinegar. Add to broccoli mixture and toss well.

Chill well before serving.

Makes 8 to 10 servings

SALAD

3 pounds broccoli flowerets
½ white onion, diced
⅔ pound cheddar cheese, shredded
1⅔ cups cooked crumbled bacon

DRESSING

3⅓ cups mayonnaise
5 tablespoons sugar
1 tablespoon white vinegar

Spinach Rice Salad

2 6- to 7-ounce boxes rice pilaf mix
2 cups packed fresh spinach leaves, shredded coarse
2 green onions, cut into rings
1 cup sliced mushrooms
4 strips bacon, cooked and crumbled
⅔ cup prepared Italian dressing
1½ tablespoons soy sauce
1 tablespoon fresh lemon juice

Prepare pilaf according to directions on package. Set aside to cool.

Place cooled pilaf in a mixing bowl. Add spinach, green onion, mushrooms, and bacon. Toss lightly.

In another bowl, mix the Italian dressing, soy sauce, and lemon juice. Add to rice mixture and mix well.

Chill well before serving.

Makes 8 servings

Traditional Greek Salad

In a small dish, stir dry mustard and water together. Let stand 10 minutes.

In a jar with a tight-fitting lid, combine all dressing ingredients. Shake well. Set aside.

Toss greens and spinach together and divide among 4 large salad plates. Cut tomato into wedges, then cut each wedge in half crosswise.

Arrange a portion of tomato, cucumber, hot peppers, olives, red onion, and beets over each salad. Sprinkle feta and pepper over all.

Add dressing to taste and toss at table.

Makes 4 servings

DRESSING

½ teaspoon dry mustard
½ teaspoon water
¾ cup extra-virgin olive oil
4½ tablespoons red wine vinegar
2¼ teaspoons dried oregano
½ teaspoon salt
¼ teaspoon garlic powder
¼ teaspoon pepper

SALAD

6 cups torn mixed greens
2 cups fresh spinach, trimmed
1 large tomato
1 small cucumber, sliced
4 pickled hot peppers, such as sport peppers
12 black Greek olives
4 thin slices red onion, separated into rings
12 slices cooked beets
2 cups (8 ounces) crumbled feta cheese
Pepper to taste

Pasta Primavera

SALAD
1 pound fettuccine
2 cups broccoli flowerets
1 tablespoon extra-virgin olive oil
1 cup (4 ounces) grated Parmesan cheese
2 tomatoes, cut into wedges
1 carrot, cut into slivers
½ cup sliced zucchini
½ cup chopped celery
½ cup sliced green onion
½ cup sliced pitted black olives
¼ cup slivered red onion
1 tablespoon diced pimiento

DRESSING
½ cup extra-virgin olive oil
2 tablespoons red wine vinegar
1 cup chopped fresh parsley
1½ teaspoons dried basil
½ teaspoon garlic salt
½ teaspoon pepper
Salt to taste

Cook pasta according to directions on package. About 1 minute before it is cooked, add the broccoli. Drain and toss with 1 tablespoon olive oil. Set aside to cool.

Combine the Parmesan cheese and the remaining vegetables in a large bowl. Add the cooled pasta and broccoli and toss to combine.

In a small bowl, combine the dressing ingredients. Pour over pasta and vegetables and mix well. Chill before serving.

Makes 6 to 8 servings

Lemon Pasta Salad with Basil, Tomato, and Parmesan

Cook pasta according to directions on package. Drain. While pasta is still warm, toss with lemon rind, lemon juice, and olive oil. Chill.

In a separate bowl, mix together tomatoes, fresh and dried basil, cheese, salt, and pepper. Chill.

Just before serving, toss together pasta and tomato-basil mixture.

Makes 8 to 10 servings

1 pound radiatore pasta
2/3 lemon, grated rind and juice
1/3 cup fresh lemon juice
1/2 cup extra-virgin olive oil
3 tomatoes, chopped
1 bunch fresh basil, chopped (about 1 cup)
1/4 cup dried basil
1 cup grated Parmesan cheese
2 teaspoons salt
2 teaspoons pepper

Pesto Pasta

In a large mixing bowl, combine oil, pesto, pepper, garlic powder, and salt.

Add remaining ingredients and mix well.

Chill before serving.

1 cup extra-virgin olive oil
½ cup prepared pesto
1½ teaspoons pepper
1 teaspoon garlic powder
Salt to taste
1 pound bow-tie pasta, cooked according to directions on package
1¼ cups diced celery
1 small white onion, diced
½ red bell pepper, diced
½ green bell pepper, diced
1¼ cups grated Parmesan cheese
1 cup (4 ounces) diced mozzarella cheese

Makes 8 to 10 servings

Greek Pasta and Feta Salad

Combine cooked pasta, celery, olives, and Parmesan cheese in a large bowl.

In a small bowl, combine Greek or Italian dressing, mayonnaise, oregano, and pepper. Add to pasta mixture and toss gently.

Fold in feta cheese and tomatoes at serving time.

Makes 8 to 10 servings

1 pound medium-size pasta shells, cooked according to directions on package
1 cup finely diced celery
¾ cup sliced black olives
½ cup grated Parmesan cheese
1 cup prepared Greek or Italian dressing
1 cup mayonnaise
1 tablespoon dried oregano
1½ teaspoons pepper
2 cups (8 ounces) crumbled feta cheese
2 tomatoes, seeded and chopped

五拾錢
50
10

Main-Dish Salads

Shrimp and Crab Seafood Salad *(H)*
Twisted Tuna Pasta Salad *(ML)*
Seafood Louie *(MP)*
Strawberry Chicken Salad *(D, H)*
Caesar Salad with Grilled Chicken *(D, MF, H)*
Oriental Chicken Salad with Sesame Dressing *(D, MP)*
Sesame Dressing *(D, MP)*
Mandarin Salad *(D, MF, H)*
Grilled Chicken Salad with Walnut Dressing *(D, MF, H)*
Chicken Lagoon *(MP)*
Honey Mustard Chicken Salad *(MP)*
Chicken, Walnut, and Raisin Salad *(MF)*
Tarragon Chicken Salad *(D, H)*
Club Chicken Salad with Hot Bacon Dressing *(D)*
Hot Bacon Dressing *(D)*
Curried Chicken Salad *(MF)*
Oriental Chicken Pasta Salad *(MP)*
Morocco Salad *(D, MF, H)*
Wild Rice and Turkey Salad with Raspberry Dressing *(D)*
Citrus Turkey Salad *(ML)*
Turkey Almond Salad *(MP)*
Turkey Twist *(MP)*
Smoked Turkey Salad with Jarlsberg Cheese *(MP)*
Turkey De Lite *(MF)*
Oriental Turkey Salad *(MP)*
Artichoke Rice Salad *(MP)*
Marco Polo Salad *(MP)*
Boundary Waters Salad *(D)*
Spinach Salad Supreme with Hot Bacon Dressing *(H)*
Maurice Salad *(H)*

D = Dayton's, *MF* = Marshall Field's, *H* = Hudson's,
MP = Marketplace, *ML* = Marketplace Lites

Mandarin Salad (page 56)

Shrimp and Crab Seafood Salad

Drain crab and shrimp thoroughly.

Transfer to a large bowl and combine with remaining ingredients. Chill well before serving.

1¼ pounds cooked crabmeat
6 ounces tiny salad shrimp
¾ cup diced celery
½ small green bell pepper, diced
3 green onions, cut into rings
½ cup mayonnaise
Salt and white pepper to taste

Makes 4 to 6 servings

Twisted Tuna Pasta Salad

Prepare dressing by thoroughly mixing together all ingredients. Cover and place in the refrigerator.

Boil pasta in water, without salt or fats, until tender yet firm. Drain and place in a serving bowl. Pour dressing over pasta and toss well.

Drain tuna. Place tuna, celery, onion, and peas in serving bowl with pasta and dressing and toss well. Chill well before serving.

Makes 4 servings

DRESSING

2 tablespoons plus 1 teaspoon sugar
2 teaspoons salt
2 teaspoons coarsely ground black pepper
2 cups buttermilk
⅓ cup mayonnaise

SALAD

1 pound rotini pasta, uncooked
1 6-ounce can water-packed tuna
1 cup chopped celery
⅓ cup chopped yellow onion
1 pound frozen peas, thawed and drained

Seafood Louie

Drain shrimp and crab thoroughly.

Transfer to a mixing bowl and add remaining ingredients. Toss gently.

Chill thoroughly before serving.

1¼ pounds tiny salad shrimp
12 ounces cooked crabmeat
½ cup diced celery
2 tablespoons chopped white onion
½ cup mayonnaise
¼ cup Thousand Island dressing
1½ teaspoons Cajun seasoning blend for seafood
¾ teaspoon fresh lemon juice
Salt and white pepper to taste

Makes 8 servings

Strawberry Chicken Salad

DRESSING

½ cup red wine vinegar
½ cup honey
2 tablespoons soy sauce
2 small cloves garlic, chopped
1 ½-inch piece fresh gingerroot, chopped
Salt and pepper to taste

SALAD

8 cups mixed greens
1 pint strawberries, hulled
1 tablespoon butter
1 tablespoon vegetable oil
4 skinned and boned chicken breast halves, cut into strips
½ cup chopped walnuts
4 sprigs parsley

Combine all dressing ingredients and set aside.

Divide greens among 4 large salad plates and set them in the refrigerator while you make the salad. Reserve 4 large whole berries to use as garnish. Cut the remaining berries in half.

Melt the butter with the oil in a large skillet. Add the chicken and cook over high heat 4 to 5 minutes until meat is no longer pink. Add ¾ cup of the dressing and cook 30 seconds. Add the halved berries and cook 30 seconds just until they are heated.

Spoon chicken and berries over greens and sprinkle with walnuts. Garnish each plate with a whole berry and a sprig of parsley.

Makes 4 servings

Caesar Salad with Grilled Chicken

¼ cup olive oil
2 large cloves garlic, minced
4 skinned and boned chicken breast halves
Seasoned salt to taste
8 to 10 cups romaine lettuce, torn into bite-sized pieces
4 sun-dried tomatoes, cut into slivers
1 cup prepared Caesar dressing
8 anchovies
¾ cup croutons
¼ cup (1 ounce) grated Parmesan cheese
Coarsely ground black pepper to taste

Combine olive oil and garlic in a small dish. Brush over chicken and season chicken with seasoned salt. Grill or broil about 8 minutes until cooked. Cut into strips.

Toss lettuce and sun-dried tomatoes with dressing to taste. Divide among 4 large salad plates. Arrange a portion of chicken over each plate. Crisscross anchovies on top of chicken.

Sprinkle each salad with croutons and Parmesan cheese and serve with freshly ground pepper.

Makes 4 servings

Oriental Chicken Salad with Sesame Dressing

4 skinned and boned chicken breast halves
Salt and pepper to taste
⅞ cup Oriental Sesame Dressing (see page 55 for recipe)
1 large head iceberg lettuce, torn into pieces
3 cups thinly sliced mushrooms
4 green onions, cut into rings
1 6-ounce box frozen pea pods, thawed and patted dry
1 tablespoon sesame seeds
1 8-ounce can mandarin orange sections, drained
Fried Wontons (see page 137 for recipe)

Preheat oven to 350°F.

Arrange chicken in a small baking pan and add salt and pepper. Cover with aluminum foil. Bake 25 to 30 minutes until juices run clear instead of pink. While still warm, shred chicken and toss with ⅓ cup Sesame Dressing. Refrigerate until well chilled.

In a large bowl, toss together lettuce, mushrooms, green onion, pea pods, and sesame seeds. Add Sesame Dressing to taste and toss well. Divide among 4 large salad plates and top with a portion of chicken.

Garnish with mandarin orange sections and Fried Wontons.

Makes 4 servings

Oriental Sesame Dressing

Using a food processor, blend together egg yolk, soy sauce, vinegar, and sugar. Add sesame oil, vegetable oil, and pepper. Blend for 30 seconds. Keep refrigerated.

Makes 2½ cups

1 egg yolk
¼ cup soy sauce
¼ cup rice vinegar
¼ cup sugar
1 cup sesame oil
½ cup vegetable oil
¼ teaspoon pepper

Mandarin Salad

To marinate the chicken, combine soy sauce, orange juice, half the green onion, and garlic in a large plastic food bag. Add chicken, seal, and refrigerate at least 30 minutes or overnight.

CHICKEN AND MARINADE

½ cup soy sauce
¼ cup orange juice
4 green onions, cut into rings
1 small clove garlic, minced
1 pound skinned and boned chicken breast meat

DRESSING

⅓ cup sugar
3 tablespoons cider vinegar
2¼ teaspoons onion juice
1 teaspoon soy sauce
½ teaspoon dry mustard
Salt to taste
½ cup vegetable oil
2¼ teaspoons toasted sesame seeds

Grill or broil chicken until cooked. Chill thoroughly, then cut into strips.

To make the dressing, combine sugar, vinegar, onion juice, soy sauce, mustard, and salt in a medium bowl. Start mixing with an electric mixer on medium speed. Slowly add oil and mix until thick. Add sesame seeds and beat thoroughly. Set aside.

Combine chicken, bacon, red pepper, water chestnuts, orange sections, pea pods, remaining green onion, romaine lettuce, and iceberg lettuce in a large bowl. Add ¾ cup of the dressing and toss lightly. Add wontons and toss again.

Line a large salad bowl with leaf lettuce. Add salad and garnish with almonds and sesame seeds.

Makes 4 servings

SALAD

5 strips bacon, cooked and chopped
5 tablespoons diced canned roasted red peppers
1 8-ounce can sliced water chestnuts, drained
1 11-ounce can mandarin orange sections, drained
1 cup frozen pea pods, thawed and patted dry
2½ cups ½-inch slices romaine lettuce
2½ cups ½-inch slices iceberg lettuce
1 cup Fried Wontons (see page 137 for recipe)
Red or green leaf lettuce to line bowl
¼ cup toasted sliced almonds
5 teaspoons toasted sesame seeds

Grilled Chicken Salad with Walnut Dressing

Preheat oven to 350°F.

Combine vinegar, mustard, garlic, salt, and pepper in a bowl, mixing well. Whisk in oil. Set aside.

Spread pine nuts on a baking sheet. Bake 8 to 10 minutes, stirring several times, just until they are light brown and fragrant. Set aside.

Combine herbs in a small dish and set aside.

Divide greens and tomato slices among 4 large salad plates.

Heat oil in a large skillet. Add chicken, seasoned salt, and 1 tablespoon of the mixed herbs. Cook over high heat 4 to 5 minutes until meat is no longer pink.

Spoon chicken over greens and add dressing to taste. Sprinkle remaining herbs and toasted pine nuts over each salad.

WALNUT DRESSING

¼ cup red wine vinegar
¼ cup Dijon mustard
2 medium cloves garlic, minced
1 teaspoon salt
1 teaspoon pepper
¾ cup walnut oil

SALAD

¼ cup pine nuts
3 tablespoons minced fresh parsley
3 tablespoons minced fresh tarragon
3 tablespoons snipped fresh or dried chives
8–10 cups mixed greens
12 slices tomato
¼ cup olive oil
4 skinned and boned chicken breast halves, cut into strips
Seasoned salt to taste

Makes 4 servings

Grilled Chicken Salad with Walnut Dressing

Chicken Lagoon

Preheat oven to 350°F.

Stir together the mayonnaise, sour cream, apple juice, cinnamon, garlic salt, and pepper. Set aside.

DRESSING
1 cup mayonnaise
⅓ cup sour cream
⅓ cup apple juice
1 teaspoon cinnamon
1 teaspoon garlic salt
Pepper to taste

SALAD
1 cup wild rice
½ cup sliced almonds
1 pound cooked chicken breast meat, torn into pieces
½ cup diced celery
½ cup sliced water chestnuts
1 small Granny Smith apple with peel, diced fine
1 cup seedless red grapes

Cook rice according to directions on package. Set aside to cool.

Spread almonds on a baking sheet. Bake 8 to 10 minutes until they are light brown, stirring several times.

Combine rice, almonds, chicken, celery, water chestnuts, apple, and grapes in a large bowl. Add dressing and toss lightly.

Chill well before serving.

Makes 6 to 8 servings

Honey Mustard Chicken Salad

Combine chicken, celery, and onion in a mixing bowl.

In another small bowl, combine mayonnaise, mustard, and seasonings. Add to chicken and toss lightly.

Makes 6 to 8 servings

5 cups bite-sized pieces cooked chicken breast meat, chilled
1½ cups diced celery
2 tablespoons chopped yellow onion
¾ cup mayonnaise
6 tablespoons honey mustard
1½ teaspoons celery seed
1 teaspoon garlic powder
1 teaspoon coarsely ground black pepper

Chicken, Walnut, and Raisin Salad

5½ cups cooked chicken breast meat, cut into bite-sized pieces
1¼ cups toasted walnut pieces
⅔ cup dark raisins
¾ cup mayonnaise
¾ cup Boiled Dressing (see page 29 for recipe)
½ teaspoon fresh dillweed, crushed
½ teaspoon grated orange rind
½ teaspoon lemon juice
¼ teaspoon celery salt
Salt to taste

Toss together chicken, walnuts, and raisins.

Blend together mayonnaise and Boiled Dressing. Add dillweed, orange rind, lemon juice, and celery salt. Mix thoroughly. Pour mixture over chicken and mix well, adding salt if desired.

Chill well before serving.

Makes 6 1-cup servings

Tarragon Chicken Salad

Combine all ingredients in a large bowl and mix gently.

Chill at least 2 hours before serving. Adjust seasoning at serving time.

Makes 4 to 6 servings

4 cups cooked chicken breast meat, torn into pieces
⅓ cup diced celery
2 green onions, cut into rings
¾ cup mayonnaise
¼ cup sour cream
1 tablespoon chopped fresh tarragon
Salt and pepper to taste

Club Chicken Salad with Hot Bacon Dressing

1 pound skinned and boned chicken breasts
Hot Bacon Dressing (see page 65 for recipe)
3 small tomatoes, seeded and cut into strips
4 cups shredded iceberg lettuce
4 cups shredded leaf lettuce
2 strips bacon, cooked and crumbled

Broil chicken until done (about 8 minutes). While it is still warm, cut it into strips and place in a bowl with ½ cup Hot Bacon Dressing. Set aside to cool to room temperature.

In a large bowl, toss tomatoes with both lettuces. Divide among 4 large salad plates. Arrange chicken on top and sprinkle with crumbled bacon.

Drizzle 2 tablespoons dressing over top of each salad.

Makes 4 servings

Hot Bacon Dressing

Fry bacon until crisp. Remove the bacon with a slotted spoon and set aside. Add onion to bacon fat in pan and cook 5 minutes until onion is soft.

With a slotted spoon, add onion to bacon. Pour bacon fat into a measuring cup and add vegetable oil to equal ½ cup. Add bacon fat to cornstarch mixture and reserve.

Combine vinegar, water, sugar, salt, and pepper in a small saucepan and heat to a boil. Add cornstarch mixture and cook until thickened, 1 to 2 minutes.

Remove from heat and add bacon and onion. Use while warm.

5 slices bacon, diced
½ cup finely chopped yellow onion
Vegetable oil
2 teaspoons cornstarch mixed with 2 teaspoons water
½ cup white vinegar
½ cup water
¼ cup sugar
Salt and pepper to taste

Makes 1½ cups

Curried Chicken Salad

In a medium bowl, combine chicken, apple, celery, cashews, and raisins.

In another bowl, mix mayonnaise, Boiled Dressing, brown sugar, curry powder, and salt. Add to chicken mixture and toss lightly.

Chill well before serving.

Makes 6 to 8 servings

4 cups bite-sized pieces cooked chicken breast meat
1½ cups peeled, diced apple
1 cup diced celery
¾ cup chopped cashews
⅓ cup raisins
¾ cup mayonnaise
¾ cup Boiled Dressing (see page 29 for recipe)
1 tablespoon light brown sugar
1½ teaspoons curry powder
½ teaspoon salt

Oriental Chicken Pasta Salad

Combine pasta, chicken, pea pods, green onion, and mushrooms in a mixing bowl and toss gently.

In a small bowl, stir together Sesame Dressing, sesame oil, and pepper. Pour over chicken mixture and mix well. Chill well before serving.

Makes 6 to 8 servings

8 ounces fusilli pasta, cooked according to directions on package
2 cups (8 ounces) cooked, shredded chicken
4 ounces (2 cups) fresh pea pods, blanched and halved lengthwise
4 green onions, cut into rings
1½ cups thinly sliced mushrooms
⅞ cup Oriental Sesame Dressing (see page 55 for recipe)
1 teaspoon sesame oil
Pepper to taste

Morocco Salad

SALAD
2 tablespoons butter
4 chicken breast halves, skinned, boned, and diced
4 teaspoons curry powder
1 small carrot, cut into thin strips
½ red bell pepper, cut into thin strips
½ small red onion, cut into thin strips
4 artichoke hearts, quartered
2 cups Couscous (see page 138 for recipe)
¼ cup dark raisins
2 tablespoons chopped fresh parsley

DRESSING
2 cups (16 ounces) plain yogurt
¼ cup orange juice
2 tablespoons honey

Melt butter in a large skillet. Add chicken and cook until no longer pink. Add curry powder, carrot, red pepper, onion, and artichoke hearts. Cook, stirring often, 4 to 5 minutes until vegetables are tender. Remove from heat and fold in Couscous, raisins, and parsley. Chill well.

For dressing, combine all ingredients. Serve with salad, passing separately.

Makes 4 to 6 servings

MOROCCO
5888

Wild Rice and Turkey Salad with Raspberry Dressing

To make the dressing, combine vinegar, sugar, pepper, and salt. Mix well until sugar dissolves. Whisk in oil. Set aside.

Cook rice according to directions on package.

When cool, combine with turkey, spinach, mushrooms, green onion, and tomatoes. Add dressing and toss lightly.

Chill well before serving.

Makes 6 servings

RASPBERRY DRESSING

½ cup raspberry vinegar
1 tablespoon sugar
1½ teaspoons coarsely ground black pepper
Salt to taste
½ cup vegetable oil

SALAD

1½ cups wild rice
1 pound cooked turkey breast meat, torn into pieces
2 cups packed fresh spinach leaves, slivered
1 cup sliced mushrooms
4 green onions, cut into rings
1 cup halved cherry tomatoes

Citrus Turkey Salad

Combine mayonnaise, yogurt, lemon juice, and curry powder in a large bowl. Add turkey, orange sections, melon, celery, and walnuts. Mix well.

Chill thoroughly before serving.

Makes 4 servings

¼ cup reduced-calorie mayonnaise
¼ cup plain yogurt
1 teaspoon fresh lemon juice
½ teaspoon curry powder
12 ounces cooked turkey breast meat, diced
1 11-ounce can mandarin orange sections, drained
¼ medium-size ripe honeydew melon, peeled, seeded, and diced
¼ cup diced celery
2 tablespoons chopped walnuts

Turkey Almond Salad

Preheat oven to 350°F.

Spread the almonds on a baking sheet. Bake 8 to 10 minutes, stirring several times, until they are light brown and fragrant. Set aside to cool.

1½ cups slivered almonds
6 cups cooked turkey breast meat, torn into pieces
3 cups diced celery
1½ cups mayonnaise
½ cup sour cream
2 tablespoons fresh lemon juice
1½ teaspoons coarsely ground black pepper

Combine almonds, turkey, and celery in a mixing bowl. Add mayonnaise, sour cream, lemon juice, and pepper. Toss gently.

Refrigerate until well chilled.

Makes 8 servings

Turkey Twist

Combine turkey, pasta, cucumber, celery, onion, and olives in a large bowl.

In a small bowl, combine mayonnaise, Italian dressing, lemon juice, mustard, salt, and pepper. Add to turkey mixture and toss lightly.

Chill well before serving.

Makes 6 to 8 servings

- *2 cups (8 ounces) cooked turkey breast meat, torn into pieces*
- *8 ounces rotini pasta, cooked according to directions on package*
- *1 large cucumber, seeded and diced*
- *½ cup diced celery*
- *½ small white onion, diced*
- *⅓ cup sliced black olives*
- *1¼ cups mayonnaise*
- *½ cup prepared Italian dressing*
- *1 tablespoon fresh lemon juice*
- *1½ teaspoons Dijon mustard*
- *Salt and pepper to taste*

Smoked Turkey Salad with Jarlsberg Cheese

4 cups (1 pound) smoked turkey breast meat, torn into pieces
¾ cup (3 ounces) diced Jarlsberg cheese
1½ cups seedless red grapes
1 cup diced celery
1 cup mayonnaise
¼ cup raspberry vinegar
1 tablespoon crushed green peppercorns
Salt and black pepper to taste

Combine turkey, cheese, grapes, and celery in a mixing bowl. Add the mayonnaise, vinegar, peppercorns, salt, and black pepper and mix gently.

Chill well before serving.

Makes 4 to 6 servings

Turkey De Lite

Cook potatoes in boiling water just until they can be pierced with the tip of a knife. Remove from heat and drain. When they are cool enough to handle, dice potatoes and place in a bowl with the turkey, celery, green onion, red pepper, and parsley.

In a small bowl, combine the yogurt, mayonnaise, mustard, and pepper. Add to salad and toss lightly.

Chill well before serving.

Makes 12 servings

3 pounds tiny red new potatoes
5 cups (1¼ pounds) cooked turkey breast meat, torn into pieces
½ cup diced celery
½ cup sliced green onion
½ cup diced red bell pepper
2 tablespoons chopped fresh parsley
¾ cup plain low-fat yogurt
¾ cup reduced-calorie mayonnaise
¼ cup Dijon mustard
¼ teaspoon coarsely ground black pepper

Oriental Turkey Salad

Preheat oven to 350°F.

Spread sesame seeds on a baking sheet. Bake 6 to 8 minutes just until they begin to color. Stir them several times and watch carefully so they do not burn.

2 tablespoons sesame seeds
8 ounces spaghetti, cooked according to directions on package
2 cups (8 ounces) cooked turkey breast meat, torn into pieces
3 green onions, cut into rings
1 large carrot, slivered
½ cup soy sauce
7 tablespoons vegetable oil
2 tablespoons smooth peanut butter
1 tablespoon cider or white vinegar
1 tablespoon sugar
1½ teaspoons ground ginger
¼ teaspoon crushed red pepper flakes

Combine cooked spaghetti, turkey, sesame seeds, green onion, and carrot in a mixing bowl.

In another bowl, combine soy sauce, oil, peanut butter, vinegar, sugar, ginger, and pepper flakes, stirring until smooth. Add to turkey mixture and mix lightly.

Chill well before serving.

Makes 6 to 8 servings

Artichoke Rice Salad

Cook rice, according to directions on package, with chicken fat or butter. Let cool.

Cut turkey into ½-inch slices. Tear slices into bite-sized pieces. Cut artichoke hearts in half. Place turkey, artichoke hearts, green pepper, onion, and olives in a mixing bowl.

In a separate bowl, combine mayonnaise and curry powder. Add to mixing bowl and combine ingredients. Gently but thoroughly stir in cooled rice. Chill and serve.

Makes 4 to 6 servings

1½ cups white rice, uncooked
2 tablespoons chicken fat or butter
1 pound cooked turkey breast meat
1 14-ounce can artichoke hearts, drained
1 green bell pepper, julienned
½ cup sliced green onion
½ cup sliced black olives
1 cup mayonnaise
1⅓ tablespoons curry powder

Marco Polo Salad

Place cooked spaghetti in a large bowl and let it cool slightly. Toss spaghetti with olive oil, vinegar, parsley, and spices. Add remaining ingredients and mix well. Chill thoroughly.

Add salt and pepper at serving time.

Makes 8 servings

1 pound spaghetti, cooked according to directions on package
¾ cup extra-virgin olive oil
¼ cup red wine vinegar
½ cup chopped fresh parsley
1 clove garlic, pressed
1 tablespoon garlic salt
1 tablespoon garlic powder
1 tablespoon coarsely ground black pepper
1 tablespoon dried basil
1 tablespoon dried oregano
1 pound Jarlsberg cheese, cut into thin strips
1 large red bell pepper, cut into thin strips
1 large green bell pepper, cut into thin strips
1 cup sliced black olives
¾ cup shredded Parmesan cheese
⅓ cup chopped walnuts
Salt and pepper to taste

Boundary Waters Salad

- 2½ cups cooked wild rice
- 1 cup (4 ounces) cooked duck meat, torn into pieces
- 2 green onions, cut into rings
- ½ cup mayonnaise
- 2 tablespoons red wine vinegar
- 1½ teaspoons Dijon mustard
- ¼ teaspoon dry mustard
- Salt and pepper to taste
- 2 small tomatoes, each cut into 8 wedges
- 2 small hard-cooked eggs, quartered
- ½ cup small broccoli flowerets, blanched
- 4 small mushrooms, halved

Combine the rice, duck, and green onion in a mixing bowl.

In a small dish, combine the mayonnaise, vinegar, both mustards, salt, and pepper. Add to rice mixture and mix well. Chill well before serving.

Serve the salad garnished with tomato wedges, hard-cooked eggs, broccoli, and mushrooms.

Makes 4 servings

Spinach Salad Supreme with Hot Bacon Dressing

1 pound fresh spinach, trimmed and cleaned
1 tomato, cut into wedges
2 hard-cooked eggs, diced
12 strips bacon, cooked and crumbled
2 cups sliced mushrooms
4 pitted black olives
4 ½-inch cubes cheddar cheese
¾ to 1 cup Hot Bacon Dressing (see page 65 for recipe)

Line a large bowl or 4 salad plates with spinach. Arrange tomato and diced egg in center.

Sprinkle bacon over the top and arrange mushrooms around the edge of salad. Garnish with olives and cheese.

Serve with Hot Bacon Dressing on the side.

Makes 4 servings

Maurice Salad

To make the dressing, combine vinegar, lemon juice, onion juice, sugar, and mustards. Stir to dissolve sugar. Add mayonnaise, parsley, egg, and salt. Mix well.

DRESSING
2 teaspoons white vinegar
1½ teaspoons lemon juice
1½ teaspoons onion juice
1½ teaspoons sugar
1½ teaspoons Dijon mustard
¼ teaspoon dry mustard
1 cup mayonnaise
2 tablespoons chopped fresh parsley
1 hard-cooked egg, diced
Salt to taste

SALAD
14 ounces ham, cut into strips
14 ounces cooked turkey breast meat, cut into strips
14 ounces Swiss cheese, cut into strips
½ cup slivered sweet gherkin pickles
1 head iceberg lettuce, shredded
12–16 pimiento-stuffed green olives

Combine ham, turkey, cheese, and pickles in a large bowl. Toss together with dressing.

Divide lettuce among plates. Top with salad and garnish each plate with 2 olives.

Makes 6 to 8 servings

Main Dishes

Grilled Tuna with Curry Vinaigrette *(MF)*

Stir-Fry Shrimp with Fennel *(D)*

Fettuccine with Smoked Salmon and Caviar *(D, H)*

Czarina Pasta *(D, MF, H)*

Shrimp and Artichoke Pasta *(D, MF, H)*

Spicy Shrimp with Pasta *(D)*

Mostaccioli with Shrimp and Feta *(D)*

Shrimp and Garlic Pasta *(D, MF, H)*

Lobster Lasagna *(D, MF)*

Andrew's Crab Cakes *(D, MF, H)*

Key West Medley *(D, H)*

Florida Chicken *(D, MF, H)*

Chicken Pie *(MF)*

Chicken and Vegetables in Herbed Cream Sauce *(D, MF)*

Bombay Chicken *(D, H)*

Yakitori *(D, MF, H)*

Chicken Pot Pies *(H)*

Chicken Focaccia with Risotto Cakes *(D, MF, H)*

The Peach Basket *(MF)*

Field's Special *(MF)*

Smoked Turkey and Avocado Sandwich with Chutney Mayonnaise *(D)*

The Epicurean *(MF)*

The Frisco Sandwich *(D, MF, H)*

Yankee Pot Roast *(D, H)*

Beef Tenderloin with Mustard Sauce *(D)*

Ginger Beef Stir-Fry *(D)*

Braised Short Ribs *(D)*

Veal Salonika *(H)*

Geschnetzeltes *(H)*

Brown Sauce *(D, MF, H)*

Meat Loaf with Red Pepper Sauce *(D, MF, H)*

Penne with Italian Sausage and Sage Cream Sauce *(D, H)*

Fettuccine Borgia *(D, H)*

River Room Soufflé *(D)*

Deep-Dish Quiche Lorraine *(D, MF, H)*

Three-Mushroom Stroganoff *(D, H)*

D = Dayton's, *MF* = Marshall Field's, *H* = Hudson's,
MP = Marketplace, *ML* = Marketplace Lites

Grilled Tuna with Curry Vinaigrette

CURRY VINAIGRETTE

1 tablespoon vegetable oil
1½ teaspoons curry powder
½ cup minced shallots
1½ teaspoons mango chutney
¼ cup chicken broth
⅔ cup crème fraîche or sour cream

4 6-ounce tuna steaks
Olive oil
Salt and pepper to taste
2 tablespoons finely diced red bell pepper
4 teaspoons raisins or dried currants
24 cooked asparagus spears
2 cups cooked Couscous (see page 138 for recipe)

Heat oil and curry powder in a small saucepan. Add shallots and cook gently about 10 minutes until they are soft.

Stir in chutney, then broth. Heat to a boil and cook about 5 minutes until mixture is reduced by one-third. Set aside to cool.

When cool, puree in a blender. Gently fold in crème fraîche or sour cream. Set aside.

Pat tuna dry with a paper towel. Brush lightly with olive oil and sprinkle with salt and pepper. Grill or broil until cooked, about 10 minutes per inch of thickness.

Spoon Curry Vinaigrette over fish and sprinkle with red pepper and raisins or currants.

Serve with asparagus and Couscous.

Makes 4 servings

Stir-Fry Shrimp with Fennel

2 large cloves garlic
1 ½-inch piece fresh gingerroot
½ teaspoon grated lemon zest
¾ cup chicken broth
1 tablespoon fresh lemon juice
1 tablespoon dry sherry
1½ teaspoons sugar
½ teaspoon oriental chili paste with garlic
¼ teaspoon crushed red pepper flakes
¼ teaspoon salt
1 pound large, peeled shrimp
2 large egg whites
3 tablespoons cornstarch
3 tablespoons vegetable oil
Fresh fennel sprigs for garnish
Lemon Pasta and Veggie Mix (see page 142 for recipe)

Mince the garlic, ginger, and lemon zest in a food processor. Add the broth, lemon juice, 2 teaspoons sherry, sugar, chili paste, red pepper flakes, and salt and mix until smooth. Transfer to a large plastic food bag, add shrimp, and seal tightly. Refrigerate at least 8 hours, turning the bag over occasionally.

Combine egg whites and remaining 1 teaspoon sherry in a bowl. Remove shrimp from marinade and dip in egg-white mixture, then roll in cornstarch.

Heat oil in a wok or a large skillet over high heat. When hot, add shrimp and stir-fry 3 to 4 minutes just until shrimp is pink. Sprinkle with fennel greens and serve with pasta.

Makes 3 to 4 servings

Fettuccine with Smoked Salmon and Caviar

Melt butter in a large skillet. Add cream and heat to a boil. Cook 1 to 2 minutes to thicken slightly.

Add salmon and cook gently 1 minute. Add pasta, salt, and pepper; toss gently. Cook just until heated through.

Divide pasta among 4 plates and garnish each serving with 1 teaspoon each of caviar, green onion, and Parmesan cheese.

Makes 4 servings

½ cup (1 stick) butter or margarine
2 cups whipping cream
4 ounces smoked salmon, cut into pieces
1 pound fettuccine, cooked according to directions on package
Salt and white pepper to taste
4 teaspoons black caviar
4 teaspoons chopped green onion
4 teaspoons grated Parmesan cheese

Fettuccine with Smoked Salmon and Caviar

Czarina Pasta

Melt the butter with the seasoning blend in a large skillet over high heat. Add the garlic, squash, zucchini, and red pepper. Cook about 3 minutes until the pepper begins to soften.

4 tablespoons butter
2 teaspoons Cajun seasoning blend for fish
2 small cloves garlic, minced
1 small yellow squash, cut into strips
1 small zucchini, cut into strips
½ red bell pepper, cut into strips
1 pound medium shrimp, peeled and deveined
2 cups whipping cream
1 pound fettuccine, cooked according to directions on package
Salt and pepper to taste
1 cup (4 ounces) grated Parmesan cheese

Add the shrimp and cook about 3 minutes until shrimp are cooked through. Add the cream and heat to a boil. Cook 2 to 3 minutes until it thickens slightly.

Add pasta, salt, and pepper, toss gently, and cook until heated through.

Serve sprinkled with Parmesan cheese.

Note: If desired, bite-sized chicken pieces may be substituted for shrimp. Follow the directions above, cooking the chicken thoroughly (about 10 minutes) before adding the cream.

Makes 4 servings

Shrimp and Artichoke Pasta

Heat olive oil, garlic, and red pepper flakes in a large skillet over medium-high heat. Add shrimp and cook 3 to 4 minutes until they turn pink.

Add green onion, artichoke hearts, cream, pesto, salt, and pepper and mix well. Add cooked pasta and heat through.

Serve sprinkled with Parmesan cheese, pine nuts, and parsley.

Makes 4 servings

4 teaspoons olive oil
2 cloves garlic, minced
1 teaspoon red pepper flakes
12 ounces medium shrimp, peeled and deveined
3 green onions, cut into rings
8 artichoke hearts, quartered
4 teaspoons whipping cream
4 teaspoons prepared pesto
Salt and pepper to taste
1 pound fettuccine, cooked according to directions on package
¼ cup (1 ounce) grated Parmesan cheese
3 tablespoons pine nuts
1 tablespoon chopped fresh parsley

Spicy Shrimp with Pasta

½ cup (1 stick) butter, chilled, cut into 8 equal pieces
12 ounces medium shrimp, peeled and deveined
1 6-ounce box frozen pea pods, thawed and patted dry
3 green onions, chopped
3 large cloves garlic, minced
1 cup shrimp stock (see Note)
1 cup seeded and diced tomato
¼ cup orange juice
1 tablespoon finely grated orange zest (colored part only)
1 teaspoon onion salt
1 teaspoon paprika
1 teaspoon dried thyme
1 teaspoon salt
½ teaspoon cayenne pepper
½ teaspoon black pepper
8 ounces spaghetti, cooked according to directions on package

Melt 1 piece of the butter in a large skillet. Add the shrimp and cook over high heat about 3 minutes until they turn pink. Add the pea pods, green onion, and garlic and cook 1 minute. Add the stock, tomato, orange juice, orange zest, onion salt, paprika, thyme, salt, cayenne, and black pepper. Heat to a boil and cook 3 to 4 minutes to reduce slightly. Reduce the heat to low. Whisk in the remaining butter, 1 piece at a time, waiting until each piece is melted before adding another. When all the butter has been melted, add the spaghetti and heat through.

Note: If you do not have shrimp stock, substitute 1 cup clam juice. Add the shrimp shells and simmer together, covered, for 15 minutes. Strain.

Makes 3 to 4 servings

Mostaccioli with Shrimp and Feta

Heat 1 tablespoon olive oil in a large skillet. Add the garlic and cook 1 minute. Add the green onion and tomatoes and cook about 4 minutes until the tomatoes start to give off some juice.

Add wine, parsley, basil, salt, and pepper and heat to a simmer. Remove from heat and set aside.

In another skillet, heat 2 tablespoons olive oil. When hot, add shrimp and cook about 3 minutes just until they turn pink.

Stir in cooked pasta and sauce and heat through. Remove from heat and gently fold in the feta cheese.

Sprinkle each serving with Parmesan cheese and garnish with a basil leaf.

Makes 4 servings

SAUCE

1 tablespoon olive oil
1 medium clove garlic, minced
4 green onions, sliced into thin rings
3 medium tomatoes, peeled, seeded, and chopped
¼ cup dry white wine
1 tablespoon chopped fresh parsley
1½ teaspoons chopped fresh basil
Salt and pepper to taste

2 tablespoons olive oil
1 pound medium shrimp, peeled and deveined
12 ounces mostaccioli or penne, cooked according to directions on package
1 cup (4 ounces) crumbled feta cheese
¼ cup (1 ounce) grated Parmesan cheese
4 fresh basil leaves

Shrimp and Garlic Pasta

¼ cup olive oil
¼ teaspoon crushed red pepper flakes
1 pound medium shrimp, peeled and deveined
½ pound asparagus, trimmed, cut into 1-inch lengths
1½ cups sliced mushrooms
½ small red bell pepper, slivered
3 green onions, cut into thin rings
1 clove garlic, minced
Seasoned salt to taste
1 pound fettuccine, cooked according to directions on package
½ cup lobster stock or chicken broth
3 tablespoons minced fresh parsley
¼ cup grated Parmesan cheese

Heat the oil and red pepper flakes in a large skillet. When hot, add shrimp and cook over high heat about 3 minutes until shrimp are cooked. Remove shrimp with a slotted spoon and set aside.

Add the asparagus, mushrooms, red pepper, green onion, garlic, and seasoned salt to the same pan. Cook, stirring often, 4 to 5 minutes until vegetables are tender but still crisp.

Add cooked pasta, stock or broth, and cooked shrimp. Heat to a simmer. Remove from heat and toss in parsley and adjust seasoning.

Serve sprinkled with Parmesan cheese.

Makes 4 servings

Lobster Lasagna

CHEESE AND SAUCE

½ cup finely diced yellow onion
5 cups ricotta cheese
4 eggs
¼ cup chopped fresh parsley
¼ teaspoon dried oregano
2 teaspoons seasoned salt
½ cup shredded mozzarella
½ cup shredded provolone
½ cup shredded Parmesan
3 cups milk
6 tablespoons butter
6 tablespoons flour
1½ teaspoons salt
½ teaspoon white pepper

Preheat oven to 350°F.

Wrap onion in aluminum foil. Bake for 15 to 20 minutes until tender. Lower oven temperature to 300°F. Mix together onion, ricotta, eggs, parsley, oregano, and seasoned salt. Set aside.

In a separate bowl, toss together mozzarella, provolone, and Parmesan. Set aside.

Scald milk in a small pan. In a saucepan, melt butter over low heat. Add flour and cook, stirring constantly, until sauce is smooth. Stir in salt, pepper, and scalded milk. Increase heat to medium and, stirring constantly, cook until sauce comes to a boil. Reduce heat and simmer for 5 minutes. Remove from heat and set aside.

Place olive oil and salt in a large pot of water. Bring to a boil. Add the lasagna noodles and cook about 1 minute until tender yet firm. Using tongs, gently remove lasagna. Rinse lasagna in cold water and place in a 9″ × 13″ pan.

LASAGNA
2 tablespoons olive oil
¼ cup salt
1 pound lasagna noodles, uncooked
8 ounces cooked lobster meat, shredded

Spread one-third of the ricotta cheese mix over pasta. Ladle 1 cup of sauce evenly over ricotta mix. Evenly arrange one-half of the lobster over the sauce. Top with one-third of the shredded cheese mix. Repeat this process twice, omitting lobster on the final layer.

Cover pan with aluminum foil and bake for 1 hour. Remove foil, increase oven temperature to 400°F, and bake for 10 to 15 minutes more until top is lightly browned. Remove from oven and let stand for 15 minutes.

Serve hot.

Makes 8 servings

Andrew's Crab Cakes

2 tablespoons butter
¼ cup finely chopped mushrooms
2 tablespoons finely chopped yellow onion
1 tablespoon finely chopped green bell pepper
¼ cup all-purpose flour
1½ teaspoons dry mustard
¼ teaspoon paprika
Dash cayenne pepper
⅔ cup whipping cream
1 large egg, lightly beaten
1 pound lump crabmeat
1 cup soft white bread crumbs
2 tablespoons dry white wine
1 tablespoon chopped fresh parsley
1½ teaspoons Worcestershire sauce
1 teaspoon seasoned salt
Pepper to taste
Flour for cooking
Butter for cooking

Melt butter in a large skillet over medium-high heat. Add the mushrooms, onion, and green pepper. Cook 5 to 7 minutes until onion is tender. Sprinkle flour, dry mustard, paprika, and cayenne over vegetable mixture and stir in. Cook gently, stirring often, for 2 minutes. Add cream and stir until smooth. Remove from heat, cool slightly, and add beaten egg, mixing well. Set aside.

In a mixing bowl, combine crabmeat, bread crumbs, wine, parsley, Worcestershire sauce, seasoned salt, and pepper. Mix well. Add vegetable mixture and combine well.

With lightly floured hands, shape mixture into patties, using about ¼ cup for large cakes, about 3 tablespoons for small ones.

Just before serving time, lightly coat both sides of crab

cakes with flour. Melt 2 tablespoons butter in a large skillet over medium heat. When hot, add crab cakes, in batches so they aren't crowded. Cook, turning once, until they are crisp and cooked through. Continue cooking cakes, adding additional butter to the skillet as necessary.

Serve hot.

Makes 8 large or 12 small cakes

Key West Medley

LIME SAUCE
1/3 cup lime juice
1/4 cup soy sauce
3/4 cup red wine vinegar
1/2 cup sugar
1/3 teaspoon cayenne pepper
1 tablespoon minced fresh mint

1/4 cup vegetable oil
3 cups raw chicken breast strips
2 tablespoons cornstarch
1 cup diced honeydew
1 cup diced cantaloupe
3 cups diced fresh pineapple
6 spinach leaves, stemmed and cleaned
2 1/2 cups cooked rice pilaf

To make the lime sauce, blend all sauce ingredients together. Set aside.

Heat oil in a large skillet. Add chicken and sauté over high heat until chicken is no longer pink. Mix together cornstarch and 1/4 cup lime sauce. Add mixture and rest of lime sauce to chicken. Add honeydew, cantaloupe, and pineapple and stir until sauce has thickened.

Place spinach leaves on a serving platter and top with rice pilaf. Pour chicken and sauce over rice.

Makes 6 to 8 servings

Florida Chicken

Combine the soy sauce, orange juice, green onion, and garlic in a large plastic food bag. Add the chicken, seal the bag tightly, and turn it over several times so the chicken is well coated. Refrigerate at least 30 minutes or up to several hours.

CHICKEN AND MARINADE

1 cup soy sauce
½ cup orange juice
1 bunch green onions, cut into thin rings
2 cloves garlic, minced
8 skinned and boned chicken breast halves

ORANGE SAUCE

1½ tablespoons butter
1½ tablespoons light brown sugar
1 cup chicken broth
½ cup fresh orange juice
1½ tablespoons red currant jelly
1½ tablespoons cornstarch mixed with 1½ tablespoons cold water
Salt and pepper to taste

Shortly before serving time, melt the butter in a medium saucepan. Add the brown sugar and cook, stirring constantly, 1 to 2 minutes, until the mixture is smooth. Add the broth, orange juice, and jelly and mix well. Heat to a boil and simmer 3 minutes. Add the cornstarch mixture and cook gently about 1 minute until sauce thickens. Add salt and pepper. Keep sauce warm while you cook the chicken.

Remove the chicken from the marinade and pat dry. Grill or broil until done, 8 to 10 minutes. Serve with the sauce.

Makes 8 servings

Chicken Pie

1 sheet frozen puff pastry dough, thawed
3 tablespoons chicken fat or butter
¼ cup all-purpose flour
2 cups chicken broth
Salt and pepper to taste
12 ounces cooked chicken breast meat, cut into strips
¼ cup tiny frozen peas, thawed
¼ cup diced cooked carrot

Preheat oven to 450°F. Have ready 4 individual casseroles with 1½- to 2-cup capacity.

Cut circles from the puff pastry to fit the tops of the casseroles. Make two 1-inch slashes in the center of each casserole.

Melt fat or butter in a medium pan and stir in flour. Cook 1 minute. Add broth, whisking until smooth. Heat to a boil and cook 1 to 2 minutes until thickened. Season with salt and pepper.

Add chicken, peas, and carrot. Divide mixture among the casseroles. Top with a pastry round, tucking the edges in.

Bake 22 to 27 minutes until puffy and golden. Serve hot.

Makes 4 pies

Chicken and Vegetables in Herbed Cream Sauce

SAUCE
2/3 cup whipping cream
1/3 cup dry white wine
1/4 cup chicken broth
2 tablespoons Dijon mustard
1 1/2 teaspoons chopped fresh parsley
1/4 teaspoon dried basil
1 small clove garlic, minced
Salt and pepper to taste

CHICKEN AND VEGETABLES
4 tablespoons butter
1 pound skinned and boned chicken breasts, cut into strips
1 pound tiny red new potatoes, cooked, peeled, and sliced
4 small carrots, peeled, diagonal-cut 1/2 inch thick, and blanched
1 cup frozen sugar snap peas, thawed and patted dry

Combine the sauce ingredients in a small bowl. Mix well and set aside.

In a large skillet, melt the butter over medium heat. Add the chicken and cook just until it is cooked through. Add the potatoes, carrots, and peas. Cook 1 minute.

Add sauce mixture and heat to a boil. Cook until slightly thickened, 2 to 3 minutes.

Makes 4 servings

Bombay Chicken

Mix together sour cream, mayonnaise, sherry, water, garlic, and lemon juice. Stir in onion and cucumber.

In a separate bowl, mix together sugar, white pepper, salt, oregano, paprika, curry powder, basil, thyme, fennel, cumin, and cayenne pepper. Blend into sour cream mixture and set aside.

In a skillet, melt butter. Add chicken and cook about 15 minutes until done. Add sauce and cook over low heat until sauce has reduced by about half.

Transfer chicken to a serving platter. Top with sauce and garnish with cucumber slices. Serve with rice.

Makes 6 servings

1 cup sour cream
¾ cup mayonnaise
⅓ cup dry sherry
¼ cup water
1⅓ teaspoons crushed garlic
1½ teaspoons lemon juice
⅓ cup chopped yellow onion
⅓ cucumber, peeled and chopped
2 teaspoons sugar
1 teaspoon each white pepper, salt, and dried oregano
½ teaspoon each paprika, curry powder, and dried basil
⅔ teaspoon each dried thyme and dried fennel
⅓ teaspoon cumin
¾ teaspoon cayenne pepper
4 tablespoons butter
6 chicken breasts
Cucumber slices for garnish
6 cups cooked rice

Yakitori

MARINADE
1½ cups soy sauce
¾ cup sugar
3 tablespoons saki or dry sherry
3 tablespoons vegetable oil
3 green onions, chopped
2¼ teaspoons chopped fresh gingerroot
1 large clove garlic, minced

1 pound skinned and boned chicken breast meat, cut into ¾-inch cubes
8 green onions, white part only
8 pieces red bell pepper, about 1 inch each
8 pieces green bell pepper, about 1 inch each
8 pieces pineapple chunks

1 tablespoon cornstarch mixed with 1 tablespoon cold water
4 cups cooked rice

Combine all marinade ingredients. Set aside ¾ cup to use for sauce.

Have ready 12 bamboo skewers. On 8 skewers, alternate pieces of chicken and green onion. On the other 4, alternate pieces of red pepper, green pepper, and pineapple. Arrange the skewers in a shallow dish in a single layer. Pour the marinade over the skewers. Refrigerate 30 minutes or longer.

Heat a grill or broiler. Broil skewers, turning as necessary, 8 to 10 minutes until chicken is cooked.

Meanwhile, heat the reserved marinade to a boil in a small pan. Add the cornstarch mixture and cook 1 minute until thick.

For each serving, arrange 2 skewers of chicken and 1 of vegetables and top with sauce. Serve with rice.

Makes 4 servings

Chicken Pot Pies

2 tablespoons plus 1 teaspoon chicken fat or butter
3 tablespoons flour
1½ cups chicken broth
¾ teaspoon salt, if desired
¾ pound cooked chicken breast meat, diced
6 4-inch prepackaged unbaked pie shells
6 4-inch prepackaged unbaked pie top crusts

Preheat oven to 400°F.

In a small saucepan, combine chicken fat or butter and flour. Stir over low heat until mixture is smooth and thickened.

While mixture is cooking, heat chicken broth in a separate pan. Add to flour mixture and beat vigorously with a wire whisk. Cook over low heat about 5 minutes, stirring constantly, until gravy is smooth. Add salt, if desired, and add chicken to gravy.

Place equal amounts of chicken and gravy into each pie shell. Top each with pie top crust. Trim edges. Bake for 23 to 30 minutes, or until pie crust is golden brown.

Makes 6 servings

Chicken Focaccia with Risotto Cakes

Place all mayonnaise ingredients in a small bowl. Mix together well and set aside.

Cut focaccia so slices are slightly larger than chicken breasts. Grill or toast. Spread each piece of bread with mayonnaise and top with a fourth of the greens, then with a chicken breast half. Season with salt and pepper. Top with Fried Leeks.

Serve open-faced accompanied by Risotto Cakes (see page 140 for recipe).

Makes 4 servings

HERBED HONEY LEMON MAYONNAISE

½ cup mayonnaise
1½ tablespoons honey
1 tablespoon chopped fresh thyme
1 teaspoon fresh lemon juice
¼ teaspoon white pepper
Salt to taste

4 pieces Herb Focaccia (see page 150 for recipe)
2 cups mixed greens
4 boned and skinned chicken breast halves, grilled
Salt and pepper to taste
1 cup Fried Leeks (see page 132 for recipe)

Chicken Focaccia with Risotto Cakes

The Peach Basket

1 Potato Basket (see page 144 for recipe)
⅔ cup Chicken, Walnut, and Raisin Salad (see page 62 for recipe)
1 teaspoon toasted slivered almonds
1 canned peach half, cut into thirds
3 sprigs chicory
2 sprigs watercress
1 canned peach half, uncut
Dollop whipped cream
1 sprig mint
2 strawberries
4 teaspoons cream cheese
1 slice Fresh Cranberry Nut Bread (see page 160 for recipe), cut into quarters

Place Potato Basket on a chilled salad plate. Fill basket with Chicken, Walnut, and Raisin Salad and top with almonds. Gently tuck peach thirds upright into basket to produce a petal effect. Place chicory around the basket and position watercress upright in the salad at the rear of the Potato Basket. Place uncut peach half on chicory. Top with whipped cream and mint sprig. Place strawberries next to peach half.

Spread 2 teaspoons cream cheese onto each of 2 quarters bread. Place remaining quarters on top of each to make finger sandwiches. Place on plate. Serve.

Makes 1 serving

Field's Special

4 large slices deli-style rye bread
1 head iceberg lettuce
8 1-ounce slices Swiss cheese
12 1-ounce slices cooked turkey breast meat
2 cups Russian dressing
4 tomato slices
4 slices hard-cooked egg
4 sprigs fresh parsley
8 pitted black olives

Cut off the bottom crust from each slice of bread. Place each piece on a serving plate.

Reserve 8 large outer leaves of lettuce. Core the lettuce and cut the head into 6 lengthwise slices. Place 1 slice on each piece of bread. (Discard other 2 slices.)

Place 2 slices of cheese diagonally on each sandwich. Top with 2 reserved lettuce leaves. Arrange 3 slices of turkey over lettuce and pour dressing over the turkey. Finish each sandwich with a slice of tomato and a slice of egg.

Tuck parsley between the tomato and the egg. Garnish each plate with 2 olives.

Makes 4 servings

Smoked Turkey and Avocado Sandwich with Chutney Mayonnaise

In a small bowl, blend together mayonnaise and chutney. Cover and chill for at least one hour.

CHUTNEY MAYONNAISE
1 tablespoon mayonnaise
1½ teaspoons prepared chutney

SANDWICH
2 slices multigrain bread
1 lettuce leaf
2 slices tomato
2–3 1-ounce slices smoked turkey
2 strips bacon, cooked
¼ cup alfalfa sprouts
¼ avocado, cut into 3 slices

Spread chutney mayonnaise on one slice of bread. Top with lettuce, tomato, turkey, bacon, sprouts, and avocado slices, then the second slice of bread. Cut on the diagonal and serve.

Makes 1 serving

The Epicurean

To make the sauce, melt butter in a saucepan. Add flour and stir over low heat until smooth. Slowly add chicken broth. Stirring constantly, cook sauce until it reaches the boiling point.

In a separate pan, warm (do not boil) cream. Stir into sauce. Add salt as desired and remove from heat. Set aside.

To make the sandwich, place one slice toast in the center of a heatproof serving plate. Diagonally cut second slice toast and place wedges on either side of whole slice. Top with ham, then turkey, then mushrooms, then sauce, then cheese. Sprinkle with paprika.

Broil about 5 inches from heat source for about 5 minutes, or until cheese is browned and bubbling. Serve hot.

SAUCE
2 tablespoons unsalted butter
2 tablespoons flour
1½ cups plus 1 tablespoon chicken broth
3 tablespoons heavy whipping cream
¼ to ½ teaspoon salt

SANDWICH
2 slices toast, trimmed and buttered
2 1-ounce slices ham
2 1-ounce slices turkey
2 tablespoons sliced mushrooms, sautéed
¼ cup shredded New York cheddar cheese
Dash paprika

Makes 1 serving

The Frisco Sandwich

Place butter, garlic, and Worcestershire sauce in a bowl. Using a mixer, whip until smooth and fluffy. Add cheese and parsley and whip for one minute more.

GARLIC BUTTER
¾ cup plus 1 tablespoon butter, softened
1–2 teaspoons crushed garlic
½ teaspoon Worcestershire sauce
1 tablespoon plus 1 teaspoon grated Parmesan cheese
2 teaspoons finely chopped fresh parsley

SANDWICH
2 slices sourdough bread
1 slice cheddar cheese
1 slice Swiss cheese
1 tablespoon butter
¼ cup sliced red onion
Dash seasoned salt
2 1-ounce slices roast beef
1½ 1-ounce slices turkey
2 slices tomato
1 lettuce leaf

Spread 1½ teaspoons garlic butter on each slice of bread. (Store remaining garlic butter in a covered container in the refrigerator.) Place bread buttered side down in a skillet and grill until golden brown. Transfer to a serving plate, buttered side up. Place cheddar cheese on one slice and Swiss cheese on the other.

Melt butter in the skillet. Add onion and sauté until tender. Add seasoned salt and stir.

Place roast beef on top of cheddar cheese and top with onion. Place turkey on top of Swiss cheese and top with tomato and lettuce. Close sandwich and cut diagonally.

Makes 1 serving

Yankee Pot Roast

½ cup vegetable oil
1 bottom round of beef, 4 to 5 pounds
1 medium yellow onion, sliced
2 large stalks celery, sliced
2 medium carrots, sliced
½ cup all-purpose flour
1½ cups beef broth
1 16-ounce can diced tomatoes
1 bay leaf
¼ teaspoon dried thyme

Preheat oven to 350°F.

Heat ¼ cup oil in a Dutch oven over medium heat. Brown meat on all sides; set aside.

Discard oil in pan and add the remaining ¼ cup. Place over medium heat. When oil is hot, add onion, celery, and carrots. Cook, stirring often, until carrots are tender, about 10 minutes. Sprinkle flour over and mix well. Cook 3 to 4 minutes, stirring constantly.

Slowly add broth, whisking until smooth. Heat to a boil. Add tomatoes with their juice, bay leaf, and thyme. Remove from the heat.

Return meat to the Dutch oven and spoon sauce over it. Cover and bake about 2½ hours until meat is tender.

Remove vegetables with a slotted spoon. Strain sauce.

Cut meat into thin slices and serve with vegetables and sauce.

Makes 8 to 10 servings

Beef Tenderloin with Mustard Sauce

1 2-pound beef tenderloin
Salt and pepper to taste
½ cup dry white wine
¼ cup Dijon mustard
1 teaspoon Worcestershire sauce
¾ cup (1½ sticks) unsalted butter, chilled, cut into 12 pieces

Preheat oven to 425°F.

Season meat with salt and pepper. Place in a shallow pan and bake until cooked rare to medium-rare. Rare will read 120°F on a thermometer and take 25 to 35 minutes. Adjust cooking time according to preference. Tent the meat with aluminum foil and let stand 10 minutes before slicing.

Just before the meat is done, combine the wine, mustard, and Worcestershire sauce in a small, heavy saucepan. Heat to a simmer. Over low heat, whisk in the butter, 1 piece at a time, waiting until each piece is melted before adding another.

Slice the meat and serve with sauce.

Makes 6 servings

Ginger Beef Stir-Fry

In a small dish combine cornstarch, sherry, soy sauce, sugar, garlic, salt, cayenne, and white pepper. Stir until smooth. Set aside.

In a wok or large skillet, heat the oil and ginger over high heat. When the oil is very hot, remove the ginger and discard. Add the beef and stir-fry just until it is no longer pink. Add the onion, carrot, broccoli, peas, and water chestnuts and cook 1 minute. Add sauce and cook until heated through.

Sprinkle with chives and serve hot with cooked rice.

Makes 4 servings

2 tablespoons cornstarch
3 tablespoons dry sherry
3 tablespoons soy sauce
1½ tablespoons sugar
1 small clove garlic, minced
Salt, cayenne pepper, and white pepper to taste
¼ cup vegetable oil
1 ½-inch piece fresh gingerroot
1 pound beef tenderloin, cut into strips
1 small white onion, sliced thin
1 cup sliced carrot, blanched
1 cup broccoli flowerets, blanched
1 cup cooked peas
1 8-ounce can sliced water chestnuts, drained
Snipped fresh chives for garnish
4 cups cooked white rice

Braised Short Ribs

6 short ribs of beef, about 1 pound each
Seasoned salt to taste
Garlic powder to taste
Pepper to taste
2 .75-ounce packages brown gravy mix
1 tablespoon butter
1 stalk celery, diced fine
1 10-ounce box frozen baby carrots
1 16-ounce can whole potatoes, drained and halved
1 8-ounce can diced tomatoes, drained
1 cup canned or frozen whole baby onions
1 bay leaf
¼ teaspoon dried thyme
¼ teaspoon garlic powder
3 tablespoons minced fresh parsley

Preheat oven to 325°F.

Place ribs in a large, shallow roasting pan and sprinkle with seasoned salt, garlic powder, and pepper. Bake for 1 hour. Meanwhile, prepare the gravy according to the directions on the package. Set aside.

Melt the butter in a medium saucepan over medium heat. Add the celery and cook about 5 minutes until it begins to soften. Add the prepared gravy, carrots, potatoes, tomatoes, onions, bay leaf, thyme, and garlic powder. Simmer gently, covered, for 5 minutes.

After the ribs have cooked for 1 hour, spill off the fat accumulated in the pan. Pour the sauce over the ribs and cover tightly. Continue cooking about 1 hour longer until meat is tender.

Sprinkle with parsley at serving time.

Makes 6 servings

Veal Salonika

3 tablespoons all-purpose flour
Salt and pepper to taste
1½ pounds lean veal stew meat, cut into 1-inch cubes
4 tablespoons butter
1 small yellow onion, chopped
1 small clove garlic, minced
2 cups sliced mushrooms
2 10¾-ounce cans cream of celery soup
1 cup sour cream
¼ cup snipped fresh chives

Combine flour, salt, and pepper. Dredge veal in mixture and set aside.

Melt the butter in a small Dutch oven over medium heat. Add the onion and garlic and cook gently 6 to 8 minutes until soft. Add the veal, in batches so as not to crowd the pan. Cook until well browned on all sides. Add the mushrooms to the meat and cook 2 minutes. Add the soup and mix well. Cover and simmer gently 45 minutes until the meat is tender. Add the sour cream and chives and cook, stirring constantly, until heated through.

Serve hot.

Makes 6 servings

Geschnetzeltes

4 tablespoons butter
½ pound mushrooms, sliced
3 green onions, cut into rings
2 pounds veal leg meat, cut into 1-inch cubes
3 tablespoons dry white wine
3 cups prepared brown gravy
½ cup sour cream
Salt and pepper to taste

Melt 2 tablespoons butter in a small Dutch oven. Add the mushrooms and green onions and cook over medium heat about 5 minutes until the mushrooms begin to give off some liquid. Set aside.

Melt 1 tablespoon butter in the same pan. Brown veal in batches, adding an additional tablespoon of butter as needed. Set the meat aside with the mushrooms. With the pan over high heat, add the wine and stir up any browned bits from the bottom of the pan.

Return the mushrooms, onions, and veal to the pan. Add gravy and sour cream and mix well. Cook gently, covered, 10 minutes until meat is tender. Add salt and pepper.

Makes 8 servings

Brown Sauce

Rub a saucepan with garlic clove. Discard clove. Melt butter over low heat. Add flour and stir until blended. Stir in bouillon.

Stirring constantly, cook sauce until it comes to a boil. Add salt and pepper and sherry or Worcestershire sauce. Remove from heat and stir.

Makes about 1 cup

½ clove garlic, peeled
2 tablespoons butter
2 tablespoons flour
1 cup beef bouillon
Salt and pepper to taste
Dash dry sherry or Worcestershire sauce

Meat Loaf with Red Pepper Sauce

Preheat oven to 350°F.

Crush the croutons and combine in a small bowl with broth. Let stand 10 minutes.

Heat oil in a skillet. Add onion and cook over medium heat 8 to 10 minutes until soft. Set aside.

In a large bowl, beat eggs. Mix in pesto, pine nuts, Worcestershire sauce, salt, and pepper. Add meat, spinach, cooked onion, and crouton mixture. Mix well.

Place loaf in a 9″ × 13″ baking pan. Bake 1 hour and 15 minutes. Let stand 10 minutes before slicing.

Melt the butter in a medium skillet. Add the red pepper and cook over medium heat 5 minutes until it begins to soften. Add the Brown Sauce, salt, and pepper and heat through.

Serve the sauce over the sliced meat loaf.

MEAT LOAF

4 ounces garlic-flavored salad croutons
1 cup beef broth
1 tablespoon vegetable oil
1 medium yellow onion, chopped fine
2 large eggs
2½ tablespoons prepared pesto
2½ tablespoons pine nuts
1½ teaspoons Worcestershire sauce
1 teaspoon seasoned salt
½ teaspoon pepper
2 pounds ground round steak
1½ cups julienned fresh spinach leaves

SAUCE

2 tablespoons butter
1 red bell pepper, diced
2 cups Brown Sauce (see page 121 for recipe)
Salt and pepper to taste

Makes 6 to 8 servings

Penne with Italian Sausage and Sage Cream Sauce

Skin and core tomatoes. Place in a strainer and press to remove excess liquid and seeds from tomatoes. Chop coarse and set aside.

2 large ripe tomatoes
1 pound bulk sweet Italian sausage
½ cup diced red onion
1 tablespoon plus 1 teaspoon chopped garlic
¼ cup chopped fresh sage
1 pound penne, cooked according to directions on package
1⅓ cups heavy cream
½ cup dry white wine
¼ cup grated Parmesan cheese
Sage sprigs for garnish

Crumble sausage into a sauté pan. Cook over medium heat 7 to 10 minutes until sausage just begins to lose its pink color. Add onion and cook for 1 more minute. Add garlic, sage, and penne. Toss. Reduce heat to very low and let stand.

In a saucepan, heat cream. Whisking briskly, add wine. Stirring constantly, cook over low heat about 5 minutes until sauce is smooth and has reduced by about one-fourth.

Stir in Parmesan. Pour sauce into pasta mixture and toss thoroughly. Transfer to a serving plate. Garnish with chopped tomatoes and sage sprigs.

Makes 4 servings

Fettuccine Borgia

Fry bacon in a large skillet. Transfer to a paper towel to drain. Discard bacon fat.

Heat olive oil and butter over medium heat in the same pan. Add the ham, garlic, and cooked bacon. Cook gently, stirring often, 5 to 6 minutes until garlic is tender.

Add cream, salt, and pepper. Heat to a boil and cook 5 to 6 minutes until cream thickens enough to coat the back of a spoon. Add the pasta and olives and cook until heated through.

Sprinkle Parmesan cheese and parsley over each serving.

Makes 4 servings

2 strips bacon, diced
4 teaspoons olive oil
4 teaspoons butter
6 ounces smoked ham, diced fine
2 medium cloves garlic, minced
2½ cups whipping cream
Salt and pepper to taste
1 pound fettuccine, cooked according to directions on package
¼ cup sliced black olives
1 cup (4 ounces) grated Parmesan cheese
¼ cup chopped fresh parsley

River Room Soufflé

7 tablespoons butter
½ cup plus 2 tablespoons all-purpose flour
2 cups whipping cream
6 large eggs, separated, plus 2 large egg whites
1½ cups (6 ounces) finely diced Canadian bacon
1¼ cups (5 ounces) shredded smoked cheddar cheese
Salt and pepper to taste

Preheat oven to 350°F. Butter a 2½-quart soufflé dish.

Melt the butter in a medium saucepan. Stir in the flour and cook 1 minute, stirring constantly. Add the cream and heat to a boil, stirring often.

Transfer the hot cream mixture to a mixing bowl and whisk in egg yolks. Fold in Canadian bacon, cheese, salt, and pepper. Set aside.

With an electric mixer on high speed, beat the egg whites until they hold soft peaks. Gently but thoroughly fold the beaten whites into the cream mixture.

Transfer to prepared soufflé dish. Bake about 30 minutes until puffy and light brown. Serve immediately.

Makes 6 to 8 servings

Deep-Dish Quiche Lorraine

1½ cups shredded Swiss cheese
⅓ cup sliced green onion
1 cup crumbled cooked bacon
1 10-inch prepackaged pie shell, unbaked
6 eggs
3 cups heavy whipping cream
1 teaspoon salt
¼ teaspoon sugar
⅓ teaspoon cayenne pepper

Preheat oven to 350°F.

Place cheese, onion, and bacon in pie shell. Set aside.

Using a mixer, blend together eggs, whipping cream, salt, sugar, and cayenne pepper. Pour over cheese mixture.

Bake for about 45 minutes, or until a toothpick inserted in the middle of the quiche comes out clean. Remove from oven and let stand for 10 to 15 minutes. Serve warm.

Note: If desired, substitute ¾ cup sautéed mushroom slices and ¾ cup cooked sausage slices *or* ½ cup cooked crabmeat and ¾ cup cooked baby shrimp for bacon and green onion. Cheddar or Monterey Jack may also be used instead of Swiss cheese.

Makes 1 quiche

Three-Mushroom Stroganoff

4 tablespoons butter
1 small yellow onion, diced
1 pound beef tenderloin, trimmed and cut into strips
Seasoned salt to taste
Pepper to taste
2 ounces shiitake mushrooms, sliced
8 ounces cultivated mushrooms, sliced
2 tablespoons red wine
1 cup whipping cream
½ cup sour cream
1 teaspoon beef base, optional
1 ounce enoki mushrooms
1 pound fettuccine, cooked according to directions on package
2 green onions, cut into ½-inch diagonal rings

Melt butter in a large skillet over high heat. Add onion and cook 4 to 5 minutes until it begins to soften. Add beef, salt, and pepper. Cook just until meat is browned but still pink in the center. Add the shiitake and cultivated mushrooms. Cook 2 to 3 minutes until the mushrooms begin to give off some of their juice.

Add the red wine and cook 1 minute. Add the whipping cream, ¼ cup of the sour cream, and beef base. Heat to a boil, then cook 1 to 2 minutes until cream thickens slightly. Fold in the enoki mushrooms.

Divide pasta among 4 plates and add a portion of the stroganoff. Garnish each plate with 1 tablespoon of sour cream and sliced green onion.

Makes 4 servings

Side Dishes

Marinated Mushrooms *(D)*

Garlic Sesame Green Beans *(MP)*

Fried Leeks *(D, MF, H)*

Fried Rice *(MF)*

Egg Rolls with Sweet and Sour Sauce *(MF)*

Sweet and Sour Sauce *(MF)*

Fried Wontons *(MF)*

Couscous *(D, MF, H)*

Wild Rice Pilaf *(ML)*

Risotto Cakes *(D, MF, H)*

Cheese and Rice Croquettes *(H)*

Lemon Pasta and Veggie Mix *(D)*

Torte à la Andrew *(MP)*

Potato Baskets *(MF)*

Rosemary Bacon Mashed Potatoes *(D)*

Garlic Mashed Potatoes *(D)*

D = Dayton's, *MF* = Marshall Field's, *H* = Hudson's,
MP = Marketplace, *ML* = Marketplace Lites

Marinated Mushrooms

Slice mushrooms and place in a serving bowl. Pour lemon juice over mushrooms. Set aside.

Mix together vinegar, vegetable oil, Worcestershire sauce, and water. Add salt, pepper, tarragon, and sugar and mix well. Stir in onion, pimiento, and parsley. Pour over mushrooms and toss.

Cover and chill for 24 hours to allow flavors to blend.

1 pound mushrooms, cleaned
1 tablespoon plus 1 teaspoon lemon juice
3 tablespoons white vinegar
½ cup vegetable oil
1½ teaspoons Worcestershire sauce
3 tablespoons water
2¼ teaspoons salt
¼ teaspoon pepper
1½ teaspoons dried tarragon
1½ teaspoons sugar
¼ cup diced yellow onion
2 tablespoons diced pimiento
2 tablespoons chopped fresh parsley

Makes 8 to 10 servings

Garlic Sesame Green Beans

Steam beans just until tender. Transfer to a bowl and add remaining ingredients.

Chill well before serving.

Makes 6 servings

1 pound green beans, trimmed
1 small clove garlic, crushed
¼ cup vegetable oil
2 tablespoons sesame oil
2 tablespoons toasted sesame seeds
2 tablespoons chopped fresh parsley
¾ teaspoon soy sauce
⅛ teaspoon pepper
Salt to taste

Fried Leeks

Trim away the green tops from leeks. Slit the white parts and fan them open, holding them under cold running water to remove the dirt. Pat dry.

2 large leeks
Vegetable oil for frying
Salt and pepper to taste

Cut leeks into very fine julienne strips about 1 inch long.

In a large, deep pan, heat several inches oil to 375°F. Add leeks in batches and cook just until they are crisp and very lightly browned, less than 1 minute. Remove with a slotted spoon and drain on paper towels. Season with salt and pepper. Hold at room temperature for up to 1 hour before serving.

Makes 2 cups

Fried Rice

Spread cooked rice on a jelly roll pan lined with plastic wrap, separating the grains as much as possible. Cover with plastic and refrigerate at least 1 hour.

3 cups cooked white rice
¼ cup vegetable oil
1 large egg, lightly beaten
¼ cup finely diced red bell pepper
¼ cup finely diced green bell pepper
¼ cup frozen peas, thawed and patted dry
¼ cup bean sprouts
2 tablespoons soy sauce
1 teaspoon sugar
⅛ teaspoon white pepper
2 green onions, cut into rings

Heat 1 tablespoon oil in a wok over high heat. When it is hot, add the egg and stir-fry just until it is set. Set aside.

Heat the remaining oil in the wok. Add the rice and stir-fry about 3 minutes until it is dry and crisp. Add the bell peppers and peas and stir-fry 30 seconds. Remove from heat and add the bean sprouts, soy sauce, sugar, and white pepper. Mix well and return to high heat. Cook 30 seconds. Remove from heat and toss in green onion and cooked egg.

Makes 6 servings

Egg Rolls with Sweet and Sour Sauce

½ pound ground pork
1 large clove garlic, minced
1 1-inch piece fresh gingerroot, minced
¼ cup soy sauce
½ teaspoon cornstarch
½ teaspoon white pepper
½ teaspoon salt
⅛ teaspoon crushed red pepper flakes
2 tablespoons vegetable oil
2¼ pounds green cabbage, shredded fine
2 medium carrots, shredded
½ pound tiny salad shrimp
½ 8-ounce can bamboo shoots, drained and chopped
2 tablespoons sesame oil
3 green onions, chopped fine
1 teaspoon five-spice powder
1 16-ounce package fresh egg roll wrappers
1 large egg, lightly beaten
Vegetable oil for deep frying

Combine pork, garlic, ginger, soy sauce, cornstarch, white pepper, salt, and red pepper flakes in a mixing bowl. Cover and refrigerate at least 15 minutes.

Heat vegetable oil in a large wok over high heat. When it is hot, add the pork mixture and stir-fry until it is cooked through. Add cabbage, carrot, shrimp, bamboo shoots, and sesame oil. Stir-fry about 4 minutes until cabbage is tender. Add green onion and five-spice powder. Cook 1 minute.

Transfer mixture to a large colander placed over a bowl. Refrigerate at least 1 hour, pressing down on the mixture occasionally to release the liquid.

Shortly before serving, place an egg roll wrapper on a flat surface with a pointed end facing you. Spoon about ¼ cup of the filling onto the wrapper, placing it slightly below the center and extending almost the whole width of the wrapper. Fold up the bottom point to cover the filling and make a half turn. Fold the sides toward the center and finish rolling up the egg roll. Brush the inside edge with the beaten egg and press it lightly to seal.

In a large, deep pan, heat 4 inches of oil to 375°F. Add the egg rolls in batches, being careful not to overcrowd the pan. Fry about 5 minutes until they are crisp all over. Transfer to paper towels to drain. Serve hot with Sweet and Sour Sauce (see page 136 for recipe).

Makes 16 egg rolls

Sweet and Sour Sauce

Combine apple cider, sugar, rice vinegar, pineapple juice, water, ginger, cinnamon, clove, and red pepper flakes in a heavy saucepan. Heat to a boil, then simmer gently 10 minutes. Add the catsup and simmer 5 minutes. Stir in the cornstarch mixture and cook 1 to 2 minutes until thickened, stirring constantly. Add the green onion and remove from heat.

1 cup apple cider
¾ cup sugar
¾ cup rice vinegar
½ cup pineapple juice
½ cup water
1 teaspoon minced fresh gingerroot
1 cinnamon stick
1 whole clove
1 teaspoon crushed red pepper flakes
½ cup catsup
3 tablespoons cornstarch mixed with 3 tablespoons water
2 green onions, chopped

Makes 3 cups

Fried Wontons

Cut wontons into ¼-inch strips. Heat several inches oil in a deep pan. When oil is hot, add wontons and fry until crisp, about 1 minute. Remove with a slotted spoon and drain on paper towels. Hold at room temperature.

6 wonton wrappers
Vegetable oil for frying

Makes 1½ cups

Couscous

Heat broth to a boil. Add butter and saffron and simmer 2 minutes.

Put the couscous in a mixing bowl. Pour boiling stock over it. Cover tightly and let stand 10 minutes.

Add parsley and fluff with a fork.

Makes 6 to 8 servings

2⅔ cups chicken broth
2 tablespoons butter
⅛ teaspoon saffron threads
1 12-ounce box quick-cooking couscous (2 cups)
2 tablespoons chopped fresh parsley

Wild Rice Pilaf

Preheat oven to 350°F.

Place water and butter in an ovenproof pot. Add rice, onion, pepper, bay leaves, and thyme. Stir well.

Bake for one hour. Remove from oven. Drain excess liquid if necessary, and remove bay leaves. Serve hot.

Makes 8 servings

6 cups water
2 teaspoons butter, melted
2 cups wild rice
2 medium-size yellow onions, chopped
1 teaspoon pepper
2 bay leaves
2 teaspoons thyme

Risotto Cakes

4 cups chicken broth
2 tablespoons olive oil
1 small yellow onion, diced fine
8 ounces arborio rice
½ cup whipping cream
½ cup grated Parmesan cheese
Salt and pepper to taste
Butter for frying

Place broth in a small saucepan and heat to a boil. Keep hot.

Heat the oil in a large saucepan. Add onion and cook gently until tender. Add rice and stir until it is well coated with oil. Add boiling stock.

Reduce heat and simmer gently, uncovered, 30 to 35 minutes until rice is tender and stock is absorbed. Immediately add cream, cheese, salt, and pepper. Mix well.

Transfer rice to a bowl and let it cool. When it is cool enough to handle, shape into 2½-inch cakes, using ¼ cup rice for each.

Melt several tablespoons butter in a large skillet. Add risotto cakes and cook, turning once, until they are heated through. Serve immediately.

Makes 16 cakes

Cheese and Rice Croquettes

1 cup long-grain white rice
2½ teaspoons butter
1 tablespoon all-purpose flour
½ cup chicken broth
5 large eggs
1¾ cups fine, dry bread crumbs
2 cups (8 ounces) shredded cheddar cheese
2 tablespoons finely chopped pimiento
Salt and pepper to taste
Vegetable oil for frying

Cook the rice according to directions on package. Set aside to cool.

Melt the butter in a small saucepan. Add the flour and cook, stirring constantly, for 1 minute. Add the broth, whisking until smooth. Bring to a boil, then set aside to cool.

In a large mixing bowl, froth two of the eggs with a fork. Add ½ cup bread crumbs, the rice, sauce mixture, cheese, pimiento, salt, and pepper. Mix well.

Froth the remaining eggs in a pie plate. Spread the remaining bread crumbs in another pie plate. Shape the rice mixture into compact ovals, using about 3 tablespoons mixture for each. Dip in bread crumbs, then egg, and again in the crumbs.

Heat 4 to 5 inches of oil in a deep saucepan to 375°F. Add the croquettes, being careful not to overcrowd the pan. Cook, turning once, until they are brown and crisp, 4 to 5 minutes per batch. Serve warm.

Makes 20 croquettes

Lemon Pasta and Veggie Mix

1 tablespoon vegetable oil
Zest of ½ lemon, grated fine
¼ red bell pepper, cut into thin strips
1 green onion, cut into rings
¼ small white onion, cut into thin rings
⅛ small fennel bulb, trimmed and cut into thin strips
½ cup thinly sliced napa cabbage
1 pound linguine, cooked according to directions on package
Salt to taste

Heat oil with lemon zest in a large skillet over medium-high heat. Add red pepper, green and white onion, and fennel. Stir-fry 2 to 3 minutes until they begin to soften. Add cabbage and continue cooking 1 minute until wilted. Add pasta and cook just until heated through. Add salt.

Serve hot.

Makes 3 to 4 servings

Torte à la Andrew

1½ pounds spaghetti, uncooked
2 tablespoons extra-virgin olive oil
1 tablespoon chopped garlic
1 medium yellow onion, diced fine
½ cup minced fresh parsley
1½ tablespoons lemon juice
2 teaspoons minced fresh basil
2 teaspoons minced fresh oregano
½ teaspoon pepper
1⅓ cups cottage cheese
1 egg
1 egg yolk
1 teaspoon garlic salt
6 tablespoons shredded Parmesan cheese
3 medium tomatoes, sliced
1½ cups shredded mozzarella

Preheat oven to 350°F. Grease and flour a 10-inch springform pan. Set aside.

Cook spaghetti according to directions on package, omitting salt. While spaghetti is cooking, heat olive oil in a skillet over medium heat. Add garlic and onion and sauté about 5 minutes until tender.

Drain cooked pasta and place in a mixing bowl. Add garlic and onion. Mix in parsley, lemon juice, basil, oregano, pepper, cottage cheese, egg, egg yolk, garlic salt, and half the Parmesan.

Press half of the mixture into the springform pan. Top with half the tomato slices, then half the mozzarella. Press the remaining half of the mixture into the pan and top with the remaining tomato slices, then the remaining mozzarella. Sprinkle with remaining Parmesan. Bake for 45 minutes.

Makes 8 servings

Potato Baskets

2 medium-size Idaho potatoes
Vegetable oil for deep frying

Peel potatoes. Using a medium shredder, shred potatoes into long strips. Cover with cold water and allow to soak for several minutes. Drain and pat dry with absorbent paper.

Heat oil to 325°F. (Oil should remain at 325°F throughout entire cooking process.) Dip wire basket form into hot oil. Let form cool to the touch.

Line the large basket of the form well with shredded potatoes, making sure that there are no thin or extra-heavy spots. Place the small basket form into the large form to hold potatoes in place.

Place form in oil, covering basket entirely. Fry about 3 minutes until potatoes are a light golden brown. Gently remove form from oil and allow to cool. Open form and remove potato basket (if basket sticks, loosen it by tapping the edge of the form with a knife). Repeat process.

Store baskets in a cool dry place for up to three days. Do not refrigerate.

Makes about 6 baskets

Rosemary Bacon Mashed Potatoes

Peel and quarter potatoes. Cook in boiling water until tender. Drain well and shake off any excess water.

Mash potatoes with a potato masher. Add cream, butter, rosemary, salt, and pepper. Whip until light and fluffy. Add bacon.

Serve hot.

Makes 4 servings

1½ pounds Idaho potatoes
¼ cup whipping cream
4 tablespoons butter, softened
1 tablespoon chopped fresh rosemary
1 teaspoon salt
1 teaspoon white pepper
2 strips bacon, cooked and crumbled

Garlic Mashed Potatoes

2 pounds potatoes, peeled and quartered
1½ tablespoons salt
½ cup whipping cream
¼ cup butter
1 heaping tablespoon chopped garlic
⅛ teaspoon white pepper

Place potatoes in 3 quarts boiling water. Add 1 tablespoon salt. Cover and boil for 20 to 25 minutes, or until tender. Remove from heat and drain. Transfer to a serving bowl.

Place cream and butter in a small pan. Heat until butter is melted. Add garlic, remaining salt, and pepper. Cook over medium-low heat until mixture begins to boil. Add to potatoes.

Using a potato masher, mash together ingredients. Serve warm.

Makes 8 servings

Breads and Muffins

Italian Bread *(MF)*

Herb Focaccia *(MF)*

Cheese Focaccia *(MF)*

Rye Bread *(MF)*

Hearty Peasant Bread *(MF)*

Old World Bread *(MF)*

Popovers *(D, H)*

Parmesan Bagel Chips *(MP)*

Croutons *(D, H)*

Fresh Cranberry Nut Bread *(MF)*

Strawberry Muffins *(MF)*

Cinnamon Crunch Muffins *(MF)*

Cinnamon Crunch *(MF)*

Frango Mint Chocolate Muffins *(MF)*

Pumpkin Muffins *(MF)*

D = Dayton's, *MF* = Marshall Field's, *H* = Hudson's,
MP = Marketplace, *ML* = Marketplace Lites

Italian Bread

1 package active dry yeast
1 teaspoon sugar
1 cup plus 2 tablespoons warm water (105°F to 115°F)
3 cups bread flour
1 teaspoon salt

Stir the yeast and sugar into the warm water and let stand about 5 minutes until mixture is foamy.

Put the bread flour and salt into a large mixing bowl and make a well in the center. Pour the yeast mixture into the center and stir to form a soft dough. When the dough is well mixed, turn it onto a floured board. Knead 8 to 10 minutes until it is smooth, supple, and elastic. Return the dough to the bowl, cover with a damp cloth, and let rest in a warm spot about 1 hour until the dough has doubled in volume.

Punch down the dough and knead it several times to remove the air. Divide dough in half and shape each half into a 12-inch-long loaf. Carefully place each loaf on a separate greased baking sheet. Cover with a damp cloth and let rest in a warm spot 35 to 50 minutes until loaves have doubled in size.

Fifteen minutes before baking, preheat oven to 425°F.

When the loaves have doubled, make 3 evenly spaced diagonal slashes across the top. Place in the heated oven and bake 25 to 30 minutes until the loaves are golden and sound hollow when tapped on the bottom.

Transfer to a wire rack and cool completely.

Makes 2 loaves

Herb Focaccia

1 recipe Italian Bread (see page 148 for recipe) prepared through the first rise
½ cup extra-virgin olive oil
1 cup (4 ounces) grated Parmesan cheese
1 tablespoon chopped fresh parsley
1 tablespoon chopped fresh basil
1 tablespoon chopped fresh oregano
1 cup (4 ounces) shredded Parmesan cheese

Divide dough in half. On a floured board, roll each half to an 11-inch circle. Transfer each one to a greased baking sheet. Brush each one all over with olive oil, then sprinkle with grated cheese, then herbs, and then shredded cheese. Set aside to rest in a warm spot for 30 minutes.

Fifteen minutes before baking, preheat oven to 425°F.

Pierce focaccia in several places with the tines of a fork. Bake 17 to 20 minutes until bread is well browned. Serve warm or at room temperature.

Makes 2 11-inch round flat breads

Cheese Focaccia

1 recipe Italian Bread (see page 148 for recipe) prepared through the first rise
½ cup extra-virgin olive oil
1 cup (4 ounces) grated Parmesan cheese
1 cup (4 ounces) shredded Parmesan cheese

Divide dough in half. On a floured board, roll each half to an 11-inch circle. Transfer each one to a greased baking sheet. Brush each one all over with olive oil, grated cheese, and, last, the shredded cheese. Set aside to rest in a warm spot for 30 minutes.

Fifteen minutes before baking, preheat oven to 425°F.

Pierce focaccia in several places with the tines of a fork. Bake 17 to 20 minutes until bread is well browned. Serve warm or at room temperature.

Makes 2 11-inch round flat breads

Rye Bread

For the sour mix, stir the yeast into the water in a large mixing bowl. Add the flour and mix well. Let stand at room temperature for at least 12 hours or as long as 24. Mixture will bubble up and increase in volume. Stir before using.

SOUR MIX
1 package active dry yeast
½ cup warm water (105°F to 115°F)
½ cup bread flour

DOUGH
1 package active dry yeast
1 tablespoon malt syrup or molasses
¾ cup warm water (105°F to 115°F)
2½ cups Bohemian rye flour
1¼ teaspoons salt
2 tablespoons solid vegetable shortening, melted

EGG GLAZE
1 large egg
¼ teaspoon salt

For the dough, stir the yeast and malt syrup or molasses into the warm water and let stand 5 minutes until foamy.

In a large bowl, combine the flour and the salt. Make a well in the center and pour in proofed yeast mixture, sour mix, and shortening. With a large, heavy spoon, stir until a dough is formed.

Turn dough onto a floured board and knead 10 minutes until smooth and elastic. Return to the bowl, cover with a damp cloth, and let rest 1 to 1½ hours until dough has doubled in volume. Punch down dough, then knead for 1 minute to remove the air.

Shape dough into an oblong football-shaped loaf. Place on a greased baking sheet, cover with a damp cloth, and let rest about 40 to 50 minutes until the loaf has doubled in size.

Fifteen minutes before baking, preheat oven to 375°F. Make egg glaze by mixing egg and salt together with a fork.

When loaf has doubled, brush lightly with egg glaze and make 3 shallow, equally spaced, horizontal slashes across the top. Bake 35 to 40 minutes until well browned. Transfer to a wire rack to cool.

Makes 1 loaf

Hearty Peasant Bread

1 recipe Rye Bread dough (see page 152 for recipe) prepared through the first rise
2 slices bacon, cooked crisp, chopped very fine
¼ cup grated Swiss cheese
¼ cup chopped almonds
3 tablespoons minced fresh parsley
Additional flour for top of loaf

Turn dough onto a floured board and knead 10 minutes until smooth and elastic. Knead in bacon, cheese, almonds, and parsley. Return dough to the bowl, cover with a damp cloth, and let rest 1 to 1½ hours until dough has doubled in volume. Punch down dough, then knead for 1 minute to remove the air.

Transfer dough to an oiled loaf pan, cover with a damp cloth, and let rest about 40 to 50 minutes until the loaf has doubled in size.

Fifteen minutes before baking, preheat oven to 375°F.

When loaf has doubled, dust lightly with flour. Bake 35 to 40 minutes until well browned. Remove from pan and transfer to a wire rack to cool.

Makes 1 loaf

Old World Bread

2 packages active dry yeast
½ cup sugar
1¼ cups warm water (105°F to 115°F)
3½ cups bread flour
¼ cup nonfat dry milk powder
1 teaspoon salt
4 tablespoons butter, melted
1 large egg, lightly beaten
½ cup dark raisins

GLAZE
1 large egg
¼ teaspoon salt
2 tablespoons coarse sugar

Stir yeast and 1 teaspoon of the sugar into the warm water and let stand 5 minutes until foamy.

In a large bowl, mix the flour, milk powder, salt, and remaining sugar. Make a well in the center and add the yeast mixture, butter, and egg. Mix well and turn onto a floured board. Knead 8 to 10 minutes until supple. Knead in raisins.

Return dough to the mixing bowl, cover with a damp cloth, and let rise about 1½ hours until dough has doubled in volume. Punch down dough, then knead for 1 minute to remove the air.

Shape dough as desired. Transfer to an oiled baking sheet. Cover with a damp cloth and let rise 40 to 50 minutes until doubled.

Fifteen minutes before baking, preheat oven to 350°F. Mix the egg and salt together.

When loaf has doubled, brush the top and sides with the egg glaze and sprinkle with the sugar. Bake 38 to 45 minutes until loaf is golden.

Makes 1 loaf

Popovers

5 large eggs
1⅔ cups whole milk
5 tablespoons butter, melted
1⅔ cups all-purpose flour
½ teaspoon salt

Preheat oven to 400°F. Grease popover pans or deep muffin tins.

Beat eggs with an electric mixer until frothy. Add milk and butter and mix well. Add flour and salt and mix just to combine.

Divide among prepared cups, filling slightly less than half full. Bake until puffy and well browned, 45 to 55 minutes. Remove from pan and serve warm.

Makes 14 to 16 popovers

Parmesan Bagel Chips

4 plain, egg, sesame, poppy seed, or onion bagels
6 tablespoons butter
1 tablespoon olive oil
½ cup (2 ounces) grated Parmesan cheese

Preheat oven to 375°F. Have baking sheets ready.

Cut each bagel horizontally into 8 thin slices. Place in a large plastic food bag.

Melt the butter with the oil; cool to lukewarm. Stir in the cheese. Add to the bag and shake the bag to coat all the slices with the butter mixture.

Arrange in a single layer on baking sheets. Bake 12 to 15 minutes until crisp and golden, turning the slices once.

Cool to room temperature, then store in an airtight container.

Makes 32 chips

Croutons

1 1-pound loaf Italian or French bread
½ cup (1 stick) butter
2 tablespoons olive oil
1 tablespoon garlic powder
3 tablespoons grated Parmesan cheese

Preheat oven to 375°F. Have baking sheets ready.

Cut the bread into ½-inch cubes and place in a large bowl.

Melt the butter with the oil. Stir in the garlic powder and cheese. Pour mixture over bread and toss so the bread is coated evenly.

Spread on baking sheets, leaving a small amount of space between the cubes so they brown evenly. Bake 12 to 14 minutes until golden and crisp, turning the cubes over once.

Cool to room temperature, then store in an airtight container.

Makes 8 cups

Fresh Cranberry Nut Bread

½ cup margarine
1½ cups sugar
2 eggs
¾ cup orange juice concentrate, thawed
4¼ cups all-purpose flour
1¼ teaspoons baking powder
2 teaspoons salt
½ teaspoon baking soda
12 ounces fresh cranberries, sliced thin
1¼ cups chopped peanuts

Preheat oven to 350°F.

Grease two 8½″ × 4½″ loaf pans. Set aside.

Using an electric mixer, beat margarine and sugar until smooth and fluffy. Add 1 egg and mix. Add the second egg and mix. Mix in orange juice concentrate.

In a separate bowl, mix together flour, baking powder, salt, and baking soda. Slowly add to mixing bowl, mixing thoroughly until just moistened. Fold cranberries and peanuts into mixture.

Place equal amounts of mixture into each loaf pan. Bake for about 1 hour, or until a toothpick inserted into the center of each loaf comes out clean. Remove from oven and let cool.

Makes 2 loaves

Strawberry Muffins

8 ounces fresh strawberries, washed and hulled
1 cup sugar
1¾ cups all-purpose flour
1½ teaspoons ground cinnamon
½ teaspoon baking soda
½ teaspoon salt
2 large eggs, lightly beaten
½ cup plus 2 tablespoons vegetable oil
½ cup chopped pecans

Preheat oven to 375°F. Line 12 muffin cups with paper liners or grease the insides of the muffin cups.

Mash the berries and 2 tablespoons of the sugar in a small bowl with a fork; set aside.

In a large bowl, combine flour, remaining sugar, cinnamon, baking soda, and salt. Mix in eggs and oil. Add strawberries and pecans and mix well.

Divide batter among prepared cups. Bake until set in center, 20 to 25 minutes. Remove from pan and cool.

Makes 12 muffins

Cinnamon Crunch Muffins

7 tablespoons butter
7 tablespoons margarine
2⅔ cups sugar
3 eggs, slightly beaten
1½ cups sour cream
1 teaspoon baking soda
6 cups cake flour
1½ teaspoons salt
1½ teaspoons baking powder
½ teaspoon nutmeg
5 cups Cinnamon Crunch (see page 163 for recipe)

Preheat oven to 350°F.

Using an electric mixer, cream together butter and margarine. Slowly add sugar and mix well. Add eggs and mix.

In a separate bowl, combine sour cream and baking soda. Let stand.

In a separate bowl, sift together flour, salt, baking powder, and nutmeg. Slowly add half the flour mixture to the creamed sugar mixture, blending well. Add the sour cream mixture, blending well. Add the remaining flour mixture, blending well. Fold in 2⅔ cups of the Cinnamon Crunch.

Grease or line 3 muffin tins with paper muffin cups. Fill each muffin well two-thirds full. Sprinkle remaining Cinnamon Crunch on top of each muffin.

Bake for about 25 minutes, or until a toothpick inserted into the center of a muffin comes out clean. Let cool.

Makes 3 dozen muffins

Cinnamon Crunch

Preheat oven to 350°F.

Combine all ingredients and mix well (mixture should resemble a streusel mix, but with larger lumps). Spread mixture evenly onto an ungreased cookie sheet. Bake for 5 to 8 minutes, or until golden brown.

Turn oven off. Let mixture remain in the oven for 2 to 3 hours to dry.

¾ cup plus 1 tablespoon butter, softened
2 cups brown sugar, packed
3⅓ cups chopped pecans
1¼ cups all-purpose flour
3¼ tablespoons cinnamon

Makes about 5 cups

Frango Mint Chocolate Muffins

MUFFINS
1 cup all-purpose flour
¼ cup unsweetened nonalkalized cocoa powder, such as Hershey's
1 teaspoon baking powder
1 teaspoon baking soda
½ teaspoon salt
⅔ cup granulated sugar
½ cup buttermilk, at room temperature
4 tablespoons unsalted butter, melted
1 large egg, lightly beaten
8 Frango Mint chocolates (about 3 ounces)

Heat oven to 350°F. Line 8 muffin cups with paper liners or grease insides of cups.

In a medium-size bowl, sift together flour, cocoa, baking powder, baking soda, and salt. Stir in the granulated sugar. Make a well in the center and pour in the buttermilk, melted butter, and egg. Stir just until ingredients are moistened.

Divide half the batter among the prepared cups. Place a Frango Mint in the center of each cup and spoon the remaining batter over each mint.

For the streusel, combine all ingredients in a small bowl. Sprinkle evenly over the muffins.

Bake until the tops of the muffins spring back when lightly pressed, 16 to 18 minutes. Remove the muffins from the tin and cool slightly before serving. To serve, cut muffins in half and spread the melted chocolate over the muffin.

STREUSEL
- *2 tablespoons light brown sugar*
- *2 tablespoons chopped pecans*
- *1 tablespoon unsweetened nonalkalized cocoa powder*
- *1 tablespoon all-purpose flour*
- *1 tablespoon unsalted butter, melted*

Makes 8 muffins

Pumpkin Muffins

2 cups all-purpose flour
2 cups cake flour
2 tablespoons baking powder
2 tablespoons salt
1¼ cups sugar
1¼ teaspoons cinnamon
1¼ teaspoons nutmeg
2 eggs
1¼ cups cooked pumpkin
1½ cups milk
½ cup plus 2 tablespoons butter, melted
1 cup dark raisins
2 tablespoons sugar for garnish

Preheat oven to 400°F.

Sift together flours, baking powder, salt, sugar, cinnamon, and nutmeg.

In a separate bowl, beat eggs slightly. Add pumpkin, milk, and butter and blend with an electric mixer. Add to dry mixture and stir until just smooth. Fold in raisins.

Grease or line two muffin tins with paper muffin cups. Fill each muffin well two-thirds full. Sprinkle sugar over top of each muffin. Bake for 20 to 25 minutes, or until muffins are golden brown and a toothpick inserted into the center of a muffin comes out clean. Let cool.

Makes 2 dozen muffins

Desserts

Lemon Soufflé *(D, MF, H)*

Carrot Cake *(MF)*

Frango Mint Liqueur Cake *(MF)*

German Chocolate Layer Cake with Coconut Pecan Frosting *(MF)*

Frango Triple-Treat Chocolate Layer Cake *(MF)*

Lemon Icebox Pie *(H)*

Key Lime Pie *(D)*

Southern Pecan Pie *(H)*

Apple Pie *(MF)*

Apple Praline Pie *(D, MF, H)*

Frango Mint Chocolate Ice Cream Pie *(D, MF, H)*

Chocolate Pecan Pie *(D)*

Cappuccino Ice Cream Pie *(H)*

Frango Mint Chocolate Cheesecake *(D, MF, H)*

Frango Toffee Marble Cheesecake *(MF)*

Crème Brulée *(D, MF, H)*

Frango Raspberry Chocolate Pecan Torte *(MF)*

Croissant Pudding *(MF)*

Ozark Pudding *(MF)*

Frango Mint Chocolate Brownies *(MF)*

Frango Mint Chocolate Chip Cookies *(D, MF, H)*

Frango Mint Chocolate Surprise Cookies *(MF)*

D = Dayton's, *MF* = Marshall Field's, *H* = Hudson's,
MP = Marketplace, *ML* = Marketplace Lites

Lemon Soufflé

3 large eggs, separated
½ cup sugar
¼ cup fresh lemon juice
1 teaspoon grated lemon rind (colored part only)
½ cup whole milk
⅓ cup all-purpose flour
⅛ teaspoon salt

Place rack in the center of the oven and preheat oven to 325°F. Butter six to seven 6-ounce soufflé dishes. Have ready a shallow roasting pan that will hold the soufflé dishes.

With an electric mixer on high speed, beat egg yolks and sugar about 2 minutes until light. Add lemon juice and rind and mix well, then add the milk. Fold in the flour and salt.

Beat the egg whites until they hold soft peaks. Gently fold into the lemon mixture. Divide among prepared dishes. Place the dishes in the roasting pan and carefully add hot water to the outside pan until it comes halfway up the sides of the dishes. Bake about 35 minutes until golden brown. Serve warm or at room temperature.

Makes 6 to 7 servings

Carrot Cake

CAKE

2 cups raisins
Hot water
2½ cups all-purpose flour
2 teaspoons baking soda
1 teaspoon cinnamon
½ teaspoon salt
1¾ cups granulated sugar
5 large eggs
1½ cups vegetable oil
3 cups grated carrot
1⅓ cups grated apple
½ cup chopped pecans

Preheat oven to 350°F. Butter a 9″ × 13″ baking pan.

Put the raisins in a small bowl, cover with hot water, and let soak for 10 minutes. Drain and pat dry.

Sift together the flour, baking soda, cinnamon, and salt. Set aside.

With an electric mixer, beat the sugar and eggs about 2 minutes until light and fluffy. With the mixer on low speed, add the oil in a thin stream and mix well. Add the flour mixture and mix just until combined. Fold in the carrot, apple, and pecans.

Transfer batter to prepared pan. Bake 40 to 45 minutes until a toothpick inserted in the center comes out clean. Cool completely.

For the frosting, cream the cream cheese and butter with an electric mixer. Add the confectioners' sugar and mix until smooth and spreadable. Spread the frosting over the top of the cooled cake.

Makes 1 9" × 13" cake

CREAM CHEESE FROSTING

1 8-ounce package cream cheese, softened
4 tablespoons unsalted butter, softened
2½ cups confectioners' sugar, sifted

Frango Mint Liqueur Cake

Place the rack in the center of the oven and preheat oven to 350°F. Generously butter a 10- to 12-cup Bundt pan. Dust the inside lightly with flour and tap out the excess.

CAKE

1½ cups all-purpose flour
1 3-ounce package vanilla pudding mix (not instant)
¾ teaspoon baking soda
¼ teaspoon salt
6 Frango Mint milk chocolates, chopped fine (about ⅓ cup)
2 ounces unsweetened chocolate, chopped fine
½ cup (1 stick) plus 2 tablespoons unsalted butter, softened
1 cup granulated sugar
2 large eggs, at room temperature
1 cup strong brewed coffee, at room temperature
½ cup Frango Mint Liqueur
¾ teaspoon pure vanilla extract

Sift together the flour, pudding mix, baking soda, and salt. Set aside.

Combine the Frango Mints and unsweetened chocolate in the top of a double boiler over simmering water. Cook, stirring often, until smooth. Cool to lukewarm.

With an electric mixer on medium speed, beat the butter until smooth. Add the sugar and increase speed to high. Beat about 2 minutes until light and fluffy. Add the eggs, one at a time, mixing well after each addition. Mix in the coffee, liqueur, vanilla, and Frango Mint mixture. Add the sifted dry ingredients, mixing just until combined.

Transfer batter to prepared pan. Bake 45 to 60 minutes, depending on the pan size, until a toothpick inserted in the center comes out clean. Let the cake cool in the pan for 10 minutes.

While the cake is cooling, make the glaze. Heat the corn syrup to a simmer. Remove from heat and stir in the liqueur.

GLAZE
1/4 cup light corn syrup
3/4 cup Frango Mint Liqueur

Confectioners' sugar for dusting

Invert the cake onto a wire rack and remove the pan. Brush half of the glaze over the cake, making sure to coat all the exposed surfaces. Let cool completely, then brush remaining glaze over cake, adding it only as quickly as the cake can absorb it. When all the glaze has been brushed on the cake, wrap the cake airtight until serving time.

At serving time, sift confectioners' sugar over the top.

Makes 1 Bundt cake

German Chocolate Layer Cake with Coconut Pecan Frosting

CAKE

4 ounces German sweet chocolate, chopped fine
½ cup boiling water
2½ cups sifted cake flour
1 teaspoon baking soda
½ teaspoon salt
1 cup (2 sticks) unsalted butter, softened
2 cups sugar
1 teaspoon pure vanilla extract
4 large eggs, separated
1 cup buttermilk

Place rack in center of oven and preheat oven to 350°F. Butter three 9-inch round layer cake pans, line the bottoms with circles of waxed paper, and butter the paper.

Put the chocolate in a small bowl. Add the boiling water and stir until chocolate is smooth. Set aside to cool to room temperature.

Sift together flour, baking soda, and salt. Set aside.

With an electric mixer on medium speed, beat the butter until smooth. Add the sugar and vanilla and increase speed to high. Beat about 2 minutes until light and fluffy. Add the egg yolks and mix well. Add the chocolate mixture. Alternately add the buttermilk and dry ingredients, adding about one-third at a time, beginning with buttermilk.

With clean beaters in a clean bowl, beat egg whites until they hold soft peaks. Thoroughly fold one quarter of the whites into the batter, then gently fold in the rest.

Divide batter among prepared pans. Bake 22

to 25 minutes until a toothpick inserted in the center comes out clean. Let cool in the pans for 10 minutes. Loosen from the pans with a small knife and invert onto a wire rack. Peel off the waxed paper and cool completely.

For the filling and frosting mixture, melt the butter in a medium saucepan. Add sugar and flour and cook, stirring often, until mixture reaches a boil. Stir the egg yolks into the evaporated milk and add the mixture to the pan in a thin stream, whisking as you add it. Cook over medium heat 8 to 12 minutes, stirring constantly, until mixture thickens. Remove from heat and add the pecans and coconut. Set aside to cool to room temperature.

To assemble the cake, place one layer on a serving plate and spread it with a thin layer of the filling. Repeat the layering with the other two layers and frost top and sides of cake.

Makes 1 9-inch layer cake

COCONUT PECAN FILLING AND FROSTING

2 cups (4 sticks) unsalted butter
1¾ cups sugar
4½ tablespoons all-purpose flour
8 egg yolks
2 cups evaporated milk
2 cups chopped pecans
2 cups sweetened flaked coconut

Frango Triple-Treat Chocolate Layer Cake

CAKE

6 Frango Mint dark chocolates, chopped fine
2 ounces unsweetened chocolate, chopped fine
½ cup boiling water
2½ cups sifted cake flour
¼ cup unsweetened nonalkalized cocoa powder
1 teaspoon baking soda
½ teaspoon salt
1 cup (2 sticks) unsalted butter, softened
2 cups granulated sugar
4 large eggs, at room temperature
¾ teaspoon pure vanilla extract
1 cup buttermilk

Place the rack in the center of the oven and preheat the oven to 350°F. Generously butter three 9-inch round layer cake pans. Line the bottom of each with a circle of waxed paper. Lightly butter the paper.

Put the Frango Mints and unsweetened chocolate in a small bowl. Add the boiling water and stir until smooth. Let cool to room temperature.

Sift together the cake flour, cocoa, baking soda, and salt. Set aside.

With an electric mixer on medium speed, beat the butter until smooth. Gradually add the sugar and increase to high speed. Continue beating about 2 minutes until mixture is light and fluffy. Add the eggs, one at a time, mixing well after each addition. Mix in vanilla and chocolate mixture. Alternately add the buttermilk and dry ingredients, adding about one-third at a time, beginning with buttermilk.

Divide the batter among the prepared pans. Bake for 15 minutes. Rearrange the pans in the oven from front to back so they bake evenly. Continue baking 15 to 20 minutes longer, until a toothpick inserted in the center comes out clean. Let the cakes cool in the pan for 10 minutes. Loosen from the pans and invert onto a wire rack. Peel off the waxed paper and cool completely.

For the frosting, melt the Frango Mints and chocolate in the top of a double boiler over simmering water, stirring until smooth. Set aside to cool.

With an electric mixer, beat the butter until smooth. Gradually add the cooled chocolate. Add the confectioners' sugar and beat until smooth.

Invert one layer onto a cake plate. Smooth about 1 cup frosting over it. Top with another layer and frost. Add top layer, upside down. Evenly frost the top and sides of the cake with the remaining frosting. Sprinkle the cake with additional chopped Frango Mints.

FROSTING

12 Frango Mint dark chocolates, chopped fine

2 ounces unsweetened chocolate, chopped fine

2¼ cups (4½ sticks) unsalted butter, softened

1 cup plus 2 tablespoons confectioners' sugar, sifted

15 Frango Mint dark chocolates, chopped fine

Makes 1 9-inch layer cake

Lemon Icebox Pie

Place the rack in the center of the oven and preheat oven to 350°F.

Whisk the egg yolks in a mixing bowl. Add the condensed milk, then the lemon juice. Transfer mixture to pie crust.

3 large eggs, separated
1 14-ounce can sweetened condensed milk
½ cup fresh lemon juice
1 9-inch graham cracker crust
¼ teaspoon cream of tartar
2 tablespoons sugar

Beat the egg whites with an electric mixer on low speed until foamy. Add the cream of tartar and increase speed to high. Continue beating until the whites hold soft peaks. Add the sugar, 1 tablespoon at a time, mixing well after each addition.

Spread the meringue over the filling, bringing it all the way to the edges. Bake about 15 minutes until meringue is pale golden at the edges. Cool on a wire rack for 15 minutes, then refrigerate at least 2 hours before serving.

Makes 1 9-inch pie

Frango Triple-Treat Chocolate Layer Cake (page 176)

Key Lime Pie

4 large eggs
½ cup plus 2 tablespoons fresh lime juice
1 can (14 ounces) sweetened condensed milk
1 prebaked 9-inch or 10-inch pie shell
1 cup whipping cream

Preheat oven to 400°F.

Beat eggs until frothy. Mix in lime juice, then milk, mixing well. Pour into pie shell. Bake until slightly warm, about 7 minutes. Cool to room temperature, then refrigerate several hours before serving.

At serving time, beat cream until it holds soft peaks. Spread over top of pie.

Makes 1 pie

Southern Pecan Pie

1 cup chopped pecans
1 rolled 9-inch pie shell
½ cup (1 stick) unsalted butter, softened
½ cup sugar
3 large eggs
1 cup light corn syrup
½ teaspoon pure vanilla extract
Pinch salt

Place rack in the center of oven and preheat oven to 450°F.

Arrange pecans over bottom of pie shell.

With an electric mixer on high speed, beat butter and sugar 1 minute until light. Add eggs one at a time and mix well. Add corn syrup, vanilla, and salt and mix well.

Pour filling over pecans. Bake 10 minutes. Reduce the oven temperature to 350°F and continue baking 30 to 35 minutes longer until pie is set. Cool to room temperature before serving.

Makes 1 9-inch pie

Apple Pie

CRUST
1 cup shortening
1¾ cups pastry flour
1 teaspoon salt
¼ cup sugar
½ cup very cold water (about 40°F)

FILLING
1 teaspoon cinnamon
4 tablespoons sugar
4 tablespoons dark brown sugar, packed
2½ teaspoons corn syrup
2 tablespoons cornstarch
⅛ teaspoon salt
2–3 Northern Spy or Jonathan apples
1 pat (1 tablespoon) butter, chilled

Preheat oven to 375°F.

To make the pie crust dough, place shortening and flour in a food processor or electric mixer. Blend together until mixture forms into small lumps. Do not overmix.

In a small glass, dissolve salt and sugar in water. Add to dough and mix until all of the water is absorbed. Do not overmix.

Roll out half the dough to a ⅛-inch thickness. Line a 9-inch pie pan with dough. Trim edges, allowing about ¼ inch of dough to hang over the edge of the pan.

Make the filling by mixing together cinnamon, sugar, brown sugar, corn syrup, cornstarch, and salt. Thinly slice apples (you will need 2 cups of slices for this recipe) and place slices evenly in pie pan. Sprinkle cinnamon sugar mix over apples. Cut butter into small pieces and place on top.

Roll out remaining half of dough to a ⅛-inch thickness. Place on top of pie and trim, allowing about ¼ inch of dough to hang over the edge of the pan. Press together top and bottom crust edges in a flute pattern.

Bake for 1 hour. Let cool until warm.

Makes 1 9-inch pie

Apple Praline Pie

4 tablespoons unsalted butter
½ cup light brown sugar, packed
2 tablespoons whipping cream
1 cup chopped pecans
1 9-inch baked Apple Pie (see page 182 for recipe)
1 cup whipping cream, whipped to soft peaks
½ teaspoon cinnamon

Preheat oven to 450°F.

Melt the butter in a small pan. Add the brown sugar and stir until smooth. Add the cream and heat to a boil. Remove from heat and add the pecans.

Carefully spread over the top of a baked pie. Place the pie in oven and bake 5 to 8 minutes until topping is browned and bubbly.

Serve the pie warm with a dollop of whipped cream and a dash of cinnamon.

Makes 1 9-inch pie

Frango Mint Chocolate Ice Cream Pie

Preheat oven to 350°F.

Butter a 9-inch pie pan. Using a mixer or a food processor, blend together graham cracker crumbs, butter, and sugar. Press mixture evenly into the bottom and sides of the pan. Bake about 8 minutes, or until crust begins to brown. Transfer to a wire rack and let cool.

CRUST
1½ cups graham cracker crumbs
6 tablespoons unsalted butter, melted
¼ cup sugar

FILLING
½ cup sugar
1½ teaspoons cornstarch
⅛ teaspoon salt
1 cup milk
8 Frango Mint chocolates, chopped fine
1 large egg, at room temperature
1 cup whipping cream
½ teaspoon vanilla extract

To make the filling, combine sugar, cornstarch, and salt in a saucepan. Add ¼ cup of milk and whisk until cornstarch is dissolved. Add chocolates and remaining milk and cook over medium-low heat, stirring constantly, until mixture comes to a boil. Remove from heat.

In a small bowl, lightly beat egg. Add ¼ cup chocolate mixture, whisking constantly until blended. Whisk egg-chocolate mixture into remaining chocolate mixture and cook over low heat, stirring constantly, until slightly thickened (about 1 minute). Do not boil. Transfer mixture to a bowl and let cool completely, stirring occasionally. Stir in cream and vanilla. Refrigerate for 2 hours.

Freeze mixture in an ice cream maker according to manufacturer's directions. Place ice cream in the pie crust and smooth the top with a spatula. Cover with plastic wrap and freeze until very firm (at least 4 hours).

To make the topping, preheat oven to 350°F.

TOPPING
2 ounces (about ¾ cup) hazelnuts
½ cup sugar

GARNISH
Whipped cream

Place hazelnuts in a single layer on a baking sheet and bake for 8 to 10 minutes, shaking the sheet a couple of times, until the skins are peeling and hazelnuts are golden brown beneath the skins. Remove from oven. Wrap hazelnuts in a clean towel and let stand for 20 minutes. Using the towel, rub off skins. (Stubborn skins can be removed by rubbing hazelnuts against a fine-meshed sieve.) Coarsely chop nuts to yield about ½ cup.

Butter a baking sheet. In a small saucepan, combine sugar and nuts and cook over medium heat, stirring constantly, until sugar begins to dissolve (about 2 minutes). Reduce heat to low and continue stirring until sugar is caramelized. Pour onto baking sheet. Let cool.

Using your hands, break the cooled praline mixture into small pieces and transfer to a food processor fitted with a metal blade. Chop fine.

Sprinkle praline on top of pie. Gently press praline into pie to adhere. Garnish with whipped cream. Serve immediately.

Makes 1 pie

Chocolate Pecan Pie

1 rolled 9-inch pie shell
3 ounces unsweetened chocolate, chopped fine
3 tablespoons unsalted butter
4 large eggs
2 cups sugar
1 teaspoon fresh lemon juice
Pinch salt
1 cup chopped pecans
Whipped cream or ice cream for serving

Place the pie shell in the freezer.

Place the rack in the center of the oven and preheat the oven to 350°F.

Melt the chocolate with the butter in the top of a double boiler over gently simmering water. Set aside to cool to lukewarm.

Whisk together the eggs and sugar. Add the chocolate mixture, lemon juice, and salt. Fold in pecans.

Transfer mixture to pie shell. Bake about 50 minutes until set in the center. Cool to room temperature, then refrigerate until well chilled before serving.

Serve with whipped cream or ice cream.

Makes 1 9-inch pie

Cappuccino Ice Cream Pie

5½ ounces chocolate wafer cookies, ground fine
4 tablespoons unsalted butter, melted
1½ pints coffee ice cream, slightly softened
1 cup whipping cream
1 tablespoon coffee liqueur
½ cup chocolate ice cream topping
Chocolate sprinkles or shavings for garnish
Whipped cream for serving, if desired

Place the rack in the center of the oven and preheat oven to 350°F. Have ready a 9-inch pie plate.

Combine the cookie crumbs and butter. Press into bottom and up the sides of the pie plate. Bake 6 to 8 minutes until set. Cool completely.

Stir together the ice cream, whipping cream, and liqueur. Pour into pie crust and place in the freezer until solid.

When it is solid, spread chocolate topping over entire surface and garnish with chocolate sprinkles. Return to freezer until serving time. Serve with a dollop of whipped cream, if desired.

Makes 1 9-inch pie

Frango Mint Chocolate Cheesecake

CRUST
¾ cup finely crushed graham cracker crumbs
1 tablespoon plus 1 teaspoon sugar
4 tablespoons unsalted butter, melted

FILLING
15 Frango Mint milk chocolates, chopped fine
3 8-ounce packages cream cheese, softened
1 cup sugar
2 large eggs
⅓ cup whipping cream
½ teaspoon pure vanilla extract

Place the rack in the center of the oven and preheat the oven to 350°F. Have ready an ungreased 8-inch springform pan.

For the crust, combine the crumbs, sugar, and butter until well blended. Press into the bottom of the springform pan. Set aside.

For the filling, melt the Frango Mints in the top of a double boiler over simmering water. Set aside to cool slightly.

With an electric mixer at high speed, beat the cream cheese until smooth. Add the sugar and beat 1 minute. Add eggs, one at a time, mixing well after each addition. Add the chocolate, cream, and vanilla and mix well.

Pour mixture into crust. Bake about 35 minutes until the sides are set but the center of the cake is still slightly soft. Remove from the oven and carefully loosen the cake from the sides of the pan with a small knife. Let cool on a wire rack.

For the topping, put the cold water in a small dish and sprinkle the gelatin over it. Transfer to the top of a double boiler over simmering water and stir until the gelatin is dissolved. Add the Frango Mints and stir until smooth. Remove from the heat and cool to lukewarm. Add the sour cream and mix well.

Carefully spread the topping over the cheesecake, cover tightly, and refrigerate at least 4 hours or overnight before serving.

TOPPING
1 tablespoon cold water
¼ teaspoon unflavored gelatin
3 Frango Mint milk chocolates, chopped fine
½ cup sour cream

Makes 1 8-inch cheesecake

Frango Toffee Marble Cheesecake

Place a rack in the center and one in the lower third of the oven and preheat the oven to 350°F. Have ready an ungreased 9-inch round springform pan. Place a roasting pan filled with hot water on the lower rack.

CRUST

1½ cups finely crushed vanilla wafer cookie crumbs
2 tablespoons light brown sugar
4 tablespoons unsalted butter, melted

FILLING

9 Frango Toffee Crunch chocolates, chopped fine
1 ounce unsweetened chocolate, chopped fine
4 8-ounce packages cream cheese, softened
1¼ cups light brown sugar, packed
4 large eggs
¼ cup whipping cream

For the crust, combine the cookie crumbs, sugar, and butter. Mix well. Press into the bottom and one-third of the way up the sides of the springform pan. Set aside.

For the filling, melt the Toffee Crunch Frangos and the chocolate in the top of a double boiler over simmering water. Set aside to cool to lukewarm.

Using an electric mixer at high speed, beat the cream cheese until smooth. Add the sugar and mix 1 minute. Add the eggs, one at a time, mixing well after each addition. Add the cream and mix well.

Pour 1½ cups of the cream cheese filling into the crust. To the rest of the filling, mix in the chocolate. Spoon large dollops of the filling into the pan. With the tip of a knife, swirl the two together to create a marbleized effect.

Bake 50 to 60 minutes until the sides are set but the center of the cake is still slightly soft. Transfer to a wire rack and cool for 10 minutes. Run a small knife around the sides of the cake to release it from the pan but leave the sides of the pan in place. Cool 1 hour, then cover tightly and refrigerate at least 4 hours or overnight before serving.

Makes 1 9-inch cheesecake

Crème Brulée

Place the rack in the center of the oven and preheat oven to 300°F. Have ready 10 to 12 6-ounce soufflé dishes, custard cups, or ramekins and a shallow pan large enough to hold them.

4 cups whipping cream
7 large egg yolks
1 cup granulated sugar
1½ teaspoons pure vanilla extract
¼ cup light brown sugar

In a microwave oven or a saucepan, scald the cream.

With an electric mixer on high speed, beat the egg yolks, granulated sugar, and vanilla 2 minutes until light. Slowly add the boiling cream and mix well.

Pour the mixture into individual baking dishes. Place the dishes in the large pan and add hot water to the outer pan so it comes halfway up the sides of the baking dishes. Loosely cover the pan with waxed paper. Bake 50 to 60 minutes until the custard is just set. Remove the dishes and cool slightly. Refrigerate at least 4 hours or overnight.

Shortly before serving, sift 1 teaspoon brown sugar into an even layer over the top of each one. Broil 6 inches from the heat 1 to 2 minutes until the sugar melts, watching carefully so they do not burn.

Refrigerate until serving time.

Makes 10 to 12 servings

Frango Toffee Marble Cheesecake (page 194)

Frango Raspberry Chocolate Pecan Torte

Place the rack in the center of the oven and preheat the oven to 350°F. Butter a 9-inch round springform pan, line the bottom with a circle of waxed paper, and butter the paper.

TORTE
1 cup (2 sticks) plus 2 tablespoons unsalted butter
15 Frango Raspberry chocolates, chopped fine
5 large eggs, at room temperature
1½ cups sugar
¼ cup raspberry-flavored liqueur
1 teaspoon pure vanilla extract
1 cup all-purpose flour
¼ teaspoon salt
1 cup chopped pecans

Melt the butter. Add the Frango chocolates and stir until smooth. Set aside to cool to lukewarm.

In a mixing bowl, lightly whisk together the eggs and sugar. Add the chocolate mixture, 2 tablespoons of the liqueur, and the vanilla and mix just to combine. Gently fold in the flour and salt, then the pecans.

Transfer batter to the prepared pan and smooth the surface with a rubber spatula. Bake about 60 minutes until a toothpick inserted in the center comes out with some moist but not wet crumbs on it. The torte will look slightly underbaked. Cool the torte in the pan for 10 minutes. Loosen the torte from the sides of the pan with a small knife, then remove the sides of the pan. Carefully invert the torte onto a wire rack and peel off the waxed paper. Sprinkle the remaining 2 tablespoons liqueur over cake. Cool completely.

For the glaze, heat the cream to a simmer. Remove from the heat and add the chocolates. Stir until smooth. Cool to lukewarm.

GLAZE

⅔ cup whipping cream
12 Frango Raspberry chocolates, chopped fine
4 ounces bittersweet chocolate, chopped fine

GARNISH

¾ cup chopped pecans
15 pecan halves, optional

To assemble, place the torte on a wire rack over a waxed paper–lined baking sheet. Spoon the glaze over the torte, letting the excess drip down the sides. With a small icing knife, smooth the glaze over the top and sides of the torte. Carefully transfer the torte to the bottom of the springform pan. Holding the torte in one hand, gently press the chopped pecans into the sides of the torte. Arrange the pecan halves over the top if desired.

Makes 1 9-inch cake

Croissant Pudding

2 tablespoons unsalted butter
4 cups whole milk
6 large eggs
⅔ cup sugar
½ teaspoon pure vanilla extract
½ teaspoon cinnamon
8 to 9 large croissants, sliced open
¾ cup raisins

Place the rack in the center of the oven and preheat the oven to 350°F. Put 1 tablespoon butter in a 9″ × 13″ baking pan and place in the oven to melt. Brush butter over sides and bottom of pan. Set aside. Have ready a shallow roasting pan large enough to hold the baking pan.

Heat the milk and remaining 1 tablespoon butter to a boil. Keep warm.

Whisk the eggs and sugar until light. Add the vanilla and cinnamon and mix well. Whisk in the hot milk.

Place the bottom halves of the croissants in the baking pan, fitting them close together but overlapping as little as possible. Sprinkle raisins evenly over them. Pour about half the milk mixture over them and let stand 5 minutes so the croissants soak up some of the liquid. Place the tops of the croissants on top and slowly pour in remaining milk mixture. Gently press the croissants into the liquid and let stand several minutes. Press them again so they are well soaked.

Place the baking dish in the roasting pan. Pour hot water into the roasting pan so it comes halfway up the sides of the baking dish. Bake 45 to 55 minutes just until the mixture is set in the center.

Cool on a wire rack for 20 minutes, then cover tightly and refrigerate at least 4 hours before serving.

Makes 8 to 10 servings

Ozark Pudding

Place the rack in the center of the oven and preheat the oven to 325°F. Grease a 1-quart casserole.

Sift together the flour, baking powder, and salt. Set aside.

⅓ cup all-purpose flour
1¼ teaspoons baking powder
⅛ teaspoon salt
1 large egg
¾ cup sugar
1 teaspoon pure vanilla extract
½ cup chopped pecans or walnuts
½ cup peeled, chopped apple
Ice cream or whipped cream for serving

With an electric mixer on high speed, beat together the egg, sugar, and vanilla 1 minute until creamy. Stop the mixer and add the flour mixture; stir to combine. Fold in nuts and chopped apple.

Transfer to prepared casserole. Bake 30 minutes until set. Serve warm with ice cream or whipped cream.

Makes 4 to 6 servings

Frango Mint Chocolate Brownies

½ cup (1 stick) unsalted butter, softened
2 ounces unsweetened chocolate, chopped fine
2 large eggs
1 cup sugar
1 teaspoon pure vanilla extract
½ cup all-purpose flour
⅛ teaspoon salt
½ cup chopped pecans
8 Frango Mint dark chocolates, chopped fine

Place the rack in the center of the oven and preheat the oven to 350°F. Butter an 8-inch square baking pan.

Melt the butter in a small saucepan. Remove from heat and add the chopped chocolate. Stir until smooth. Set aside to cool slightly.

With an electric mixer at high speed, beat the eggs for 2 minutes. Add the sugar and continue beating 1 minute until light. Blend in the chocolate mixture and vanilla. With a rubber spatula, mix in the flour and salt. Fold in the pecans and chopped Frango Mints.

Transfer batter to prepared pan. Bake about 25 minutes until a toothpick inserted in the center comes out with some moist but not wet crumbs. Do not overbake. Place the pan on a wire rack and cool completely. With a sharp knife, cut into 9 squares.

Makes 9 brownies

Frango Mint Chocolate Chip Cookies

Place two racks in the center area of the oven. Preheat the oven to 350°F. Line 2 baking sheets with parchment paper or use nonstick baking sheets.

- *2¼ cups all-purpose flour*
- *1 teaspoon baking soda*
- *½ teaspoon salt*
- *½ cup (1 stick) unsalted butter, softened*
- *½ cup solid vegetable shortening*
- *1 cup packed light brown sugar*
- *½ cup granulated sugar*
- *2 large eggs*
- *5 Frango Mint milk chocolates, chopped fine*
- *1 teaspoon pure vanilla extract*
- *25 Frango Mint milk chocolates, chopped coarse*
- *¾ cup chopped pecans*

Sift together the flour, baking soda, and salt. Set aside.

With an electric mixer, beat the butter and shortening until smooth. Add both sugars and beat 2 minutes on high speed until light. Add the eggs, one at a time, mixing well after each addition. Mix in the finely chopped Frango Mints and the vanilla. With a large spoon, mix in the dry ingredients, then the coarsely chopped chocolate and pecans.

Using a rounded teaspoon of dough for each, drop cookies onto the prepared baking sheets, spacing them about 1 inch apart.

Bake about 10 minutes until the cookies are almost set in the center. Cool on the baking sheets for 1 minute, then carefully transfer to a wire rack to cool completely. Let the baking sheets cool before using again for additional batches of cookies.

Makes 8 dozen cookies

Frango Mint Chocolate Surprise Cookies

1 cup (2 sticks) unsalted butter, softened
½ cup confectioners' sugar
1 teaspoon pure vanilla extract
2 cups cake flour
⅛ teaspoon salt
1 cup finely chopped pecans
18 Frango Mint milk chocolates, cut in half vertically

Confectioners' sugar for sifting

With an electric mixer on high speed, beat the butter until smooth. Add the confectioners' sugar and beat 1 minute until light. Mix in vanilla. Stir in the flour and salt, then the pecans. Wrap the dough in plastic wrap and refrigerate 1 hour until it is firm.

Place two racks in the center area of oven and preheat oven to 350°F. Have ready ungreased baking sheets.

Break off pieces of dough, about 1 tablespoon each. Completely enclose each Frango Mint half with dough, rolling into smooth balls.

Place cookies on baking sheets, spacing them about 1 inch apart. Bake 18 to 20 minutes until set. Cool on the baking sheets for 1 minute, then carefully transfer to a wire rack. Sift confectioners' sugar over cookies and allow to cool. Before serving, coat again with confectioners' sugar if desired.

Makes 3 dozen cookies

Index

Acorn Squash Soup, Roasted, 16
Apple
  Pie, 182
  Praline Pie, 184; *illus.*, 185
Artichoke
  Rice Salad, 77
  and Shrimp Pasta, 91
Asparagus Soup, Cream of, 13
Avocado and Smoked Turkey Sandwich with Chutney Mayonnaise, 112

Bacon
  Hot, Salad Dressing, 65
  Mashed Potatoes, Rosemary, 145
Bagel Chips, Parmesan, 158
Bean. *See also* Black Bean; Kidney Bean
  Salad, Gremolata, 36
  Salad, Mixed, 35
Beef
  Meat Loaf with Red Pepper Sauce, 123; *illus.*, 122
  Roast (sandwich), The Frisco, 114
  Short Ribs, Braised, 118
  Stir-Fry, Ginger, 117
  Tenderloin with Mustard Sauce, 116
  Yankee Pot Roast, 115
Black Bean Soup, 9
Black-Eyed Pea Salad, 38
Boiled Dressing, 29
Bombay Chicken, 105
Boundary Waters
  Salad, 80
  Wild Rice Soup, 12; *illus.*, x
Bread, 148–66. *See also* Muffins
  Cheese Focaccia, 151
  Cranberry Nut, Fresh, 160
  Croutons, 159
  Hearty Peasant, 154
  Herb Focaccia, 150
  Italian, 148
  Old World, 155
  Parmesan Bagel Chips, 158
  Popovers, 157; *illus.*, 156
  Rye, 152
Broccoli, Country Fresh Salad, 39
Brown Sauce, 121
Brownies, Chocolate, Frango Mint, 203

Caesar Salad with Grilled Chicken, 53
Cake
  Carrot, 170
  Frango Mint Liqueur, 172
  Frango Raspberry Chocolate Pecan Torte, 198
  Frango Triple-Treat Chocolate Layer, 176; *illus.*, 178
  German Chocolate, with Coconut Pecan Frosting, 174
Cantaloupe Soup, 3
Cappuccino Ice Cream Pie, 191
Carrot
  Cake, 170
  Raisin, and Nut Salad, 28
Cheese
  Focaccia, 151
  and Rice Croquettes, 141
  Soup, Canadian, 21
Cheesecake
  Frango Mint Chocolate, 192
  Frango Toffee Marble, 194
Chicken Breasts
  Bombay, 105
  Florida, 101
  Focaccia with Risotto Cakes, 109; *illus.*, 108
  Grilled, Caesar Salad with, 53
  Key West Medley, 100

Lagoon, 60
Mandarin Salad, 56; *illus.*, 46
Morocco Salad, 68; *illus.*, 69
Pie, 102; *illus.*, 103
Pot Pies, 107
and Vegetables in Herbed Cream Sauce, 104
Yakitori, 106
Chicken and Cheese Soup, 20; *illus.*, x
Chicken Salad
Club, with Hot Bacon Dressing, 64
Curried, 66
Grilled, with Walnut Dressing, 59; *illus.*, 58
Honey Mustard, 61
Morocco, 68
Oriental, with Sesame Dressing, 54
Pasta, Oriental, 67
Strawberry, 52
Tarragon, 63
Walnut and Raisin, 62
Chocolate
Brownies, Frango Mint, 203
Cake, German, with Coconut Pecan Frosting, 174
Cheesecake, Frango Mint, 192
Chip Cookies, Frango Mint, 204
Ice Cream Pie, Frango Mint, 186; *illus.*, 189
Layer Cake, Frango Triple-Treat, 176; *illus.*, 178
Muffins, Frango Mint, 164
Pecan Pie, 190
Pecan Torte, Frango Raspberry, 198
Surprise Cookies, Frango Mint, 206
Chowder. *See* Clam Chowder
Cinnamon Crunch, 163
Cinnamon Crunch Muffins, 162
Citrus Turkey Salad, 71; *illus.*, 22
Clam
Chowder, Manhattan, 11
Chowder, New England, 18; *illus.*, x
Cole Slaw, Peanut, 32
Cookies
Frango Mint Chocolate Brownies, 203
Frango Mint Chocolate Chip, 204
Frango Mint Chocolate Surprise, 206
Couscous, 138
Crab
Cakes, Andrew's, 98
and Shrimp Seafood Salad, 48
Cranberry
Nut Bread, Fresh, 160
-Peach-Plum Soup, 4
Cream Soup. *See* Soup
Crème Brulée, 197
Croissant Pudding, 200
Croutons, 159
Curried Chicken Salad, 66
Czarina Pasta, 90

Deep-Dish Quiche Lorraine, 127
Dessert, 168–206
Apple Pie, 182
Apple Praline Pie, 184; *illus.*, 185
Brownies, Frango Mint Chocolate, 203
Cake, Frango Mint Liqueur, 172
Carrot Cake, 170
Cheesecake, Frango Mint Chocolate, 192
Cheesecake, Frango Toffee Marble, 194
Chocolate Chip Cookies, Frango Mint, 204
Chocolate Layer Cake, Frango Triple-Treat, 176; *illus.*, 178
Chocolate Pecan Pie, 190

Cookies, Frango Mint Chocolate
Surprise, 206
Crème Brulée, 197
Croissant Pudding, 200
German Chocolate Cake with
Coconut Pecan Frosting, 174
Ice Cream Pie, Cappuccino, 191
Ice Cream Pie, Frango Mint
Chocolate, 186; *illus.*, 189
Key Lime Pie, 180
Lemon Icebox Pie, 179
Lemon Soufflé, 168
Ozark Pudding, 202
Pecan Torte, Frango Raspberry
Chocolate, 198
Southern Pecan Pie, 181

Egg Rolls with Sweet and Sour
Sauce, 134
Epicurean, The, 113

Fettuccine
Borgia, 125
Czarina Pasta, 90
Pasta Primavera, 42
Shrimp and Artichoke Pasta, 91
Shrimp and Garlic Pasta, 94;
illus., 95
Three-Mushroom Stroganoff, 128
with Smoked Salmon and Caviar,
89; *illus.*, 88
Field's Special, 111
Focaccia
Cheese, 151
Chicken, with Risotto Cakes,
109; *illus.*, 108
Herb, 150
Frango Mint Chocolate
Brownies, 203
Cheesecake, 192
Chip Cookies, 204
Ice Cream Pie, 186; *illus.*, 189
Liqueur Cake, 172
Muffins, 164
Surprise Cookies, 206
Triple-Treat Layer Cake, 176;
illus., 178
Frango Raspberry Chocolate Pecan
Torte, 198
Frango Toffee Marble Cheesecake,
194
Fried
Leeks, 132
Rice, 133
Wontons, 137
Frisco Sandwich, The, 114
Fruit Ambrosia Salad, 24

Garlic
Mashed Potatoes, 146
Sesame Green Beans, 131
Gazpacho, 6
German Chocolate Cake with
Coconut Pecan Frosting, 174
German Potato Salad, 31
Geschnetzeltes, 120
Ginger Beef Stir-Fry, 117
Greek Pasta and Feta Salad, 45
Greek Salad, Traditional, 41
Green Beans, Garlic Sesame, 131
Gremolata Bean Salad, 36
Grilled
Chicken, Caesar Salad with, 53
Chicken Salad with Walnut
Dressing, 59; *illus.*, 58
Tuna with Curry Vinaigrette, 86

Ham
Epicurean, The (sandwich), 113
Maurice Salad, 82; *illus.*, 83
Herb Focaccia, 150
Honey Mustard Chicken Salad, 61

Ice Cream Pie
Cappuccino, 191
Frango Mint Chocolate, 186;
illus., 189
Italian Bread, 148

Key Lime Pie, 180
Key West Medley, 100
Kidney Bean Salad, 34

Lasagna, Lobster, 96
Leeks, Fried, 132
Lemon
  Icebox Pie, 179
  Pasta and Veggie Mix, 142
  Pasta Salad with Basil, Tomato, and Parmesan, 43
  Soufflé, 168
Lobster
  Bisque, 19
  Lasagna, 96

Main Dishes, 86–128
Mandarin Salad, 56; *illus.*, 46
Manhattan Clam Chowder, 11
Marco Polo Salad, 79; *illus.*, 78
Marinated Mushrooms, 130
Maurice Salad, 82; *illus.*, 83
Meat Loaf with Red Pepper Sauce, 123; *illus.*, 122
Morocco Salad, 68; *illus.*, 69
Mostaccioli with Shrimp and Feta, 93
Muffins. *See also* Bread
  Cinnamon Crunch, 162
  Frango Mint Chocolate, 164
  Pumpkin, 166
  Strawberry, 161
Mushroom(s)
  Marinated, 130
  Soup, Cream of Fresh, 14
  Stroganoff, Three-, 128

New England Clam Chowder, 18; *illus.*, x
Noodle Salad, Timbercrest Pasta, 37

Old World Bread, 155
Oriental
  Chicken Pasta Salad, 67
  Chicken Salad with Sesame Dressing, 54
  Turkey Salad, 76
Ozark Pudding, 202

Parmesan Bagel Chips, 158
Pasta
  Chicken Salad, Oriental, 67
  Czarina, 90
  and Feta Salad, Greek, 45
  Fettuccine Borgia, 125
  Fettuccine with Smoked Salmon and Caviar, 89; *illus.*, 88
  Lasagna, Lobster, 96
  Marco Polo Salad, 79; *illus.*, 78
  Mostaccioli with Shrimp and Feta, 93
  Penne with Italian Sausage and Sage Cream Sauce, 124
  Pesto, 44
  Primavera, 42
  Salad, Lemon, with Basil, Tomato, and Parmesan, 43
  Salad, Timbercrest, 37
  Shrimp and Artichoke, 91
  Shrimp and Garlic, 94; *illus.*, 95
  Spicy Shrimp with, 92
  Three-Mushroom Stroganoff, 128
  Torte à la Andrew, 143
  Twisted, and Tuna Salad, 49
  and Veggie Mix, Lemon, 142
Pea, Black-Eyed, Salad, 38
Peach Basket, The, 110
Peach-Plum-Cranberry Soup, 4
Peanut Cole Slaw, 32
Peasant Bread, Hearty, 154
Pecan
  Chocolate Pie, 190
  Chocolate Torte, Frango Raspberry, 198
  Pie, Southern, 181

Penne with Italian Sausage and Sage Cream Sauce, 124
Pesto Pasta, 44
Pie
  Apple, 182
  Apple Praline, 184; *illus.*, 185
  Cappuccino Ice Cream, 191
  Chicken, 102; *illus.*, 103
  Chicken Pot, 107
  Chocolate Pecan, 190
  Frango Mint Chocolate Ice Cream, 186; *illus.*, 189
  Key Lime, 180
  Lemon Icebox, 179
  Southern Pecan, 181
Pilaf, Wild Rice, 139
Plum-Peach-Cranberry Soup, 4
Popovers, 157; *illus.*, 156
Pot Pies, Chicken, 107
Potato(es)
  Baskets, 144
  Mashed, Garlic, 146
  Mashed, Rosemary Bacon, 145
  New, Salad, 30
  Salad, German, 31
Pudding
  Croissant, 200
  Ozark, 202
Pumpkin Muffins, 166

Quiche Lorraine, Deep-Dish, 127

Rice. *See also* Wild Rice
  Artichoke Salad, 77
  and Cheese Croquettes, 141
  Fried, 133
  Risotto Cakes, 140
  Spinach Salad, 40
Risotto Cakes, 140
  Chicken Focaccia with, 109; *illus.*, 108
River Room Soufflé, 126
Rosemary Bacon Mashed Potatoes, 145
Rye Bread, 152

Salad, 24–45. *See also* Salad dressing; Salad, fruit; Salad, Main-Dish
  Black-Eyed Pea, 38
  Carrot, Raisin, and Nut, 28
  Country Fresh, 39
  Greek, Traditional, 41
  Gremolata Bean, 36
  Kidney Bean, 34
  Mixed Bean, 35
  Pasta and Feta, Greek, 45
  Pasta, Lemon, with Basil, Tomato, and Parmesan, 43
  Pasta Primavera, 42
  Pasta, Timbercrest, 37
  Peach Basket, The, 110
  Peanut Cole Slaw, 32
  Pesto Pasta, 44
  Potato, German, 31
  Potato, New, 30
  Seafood Slaw, 33
  Spinach Rice, 40
Salad dressing
  Boiled, 29
  Hot Bacon, 65
  Mandarin, 57
  Oriental Sesame, 55
Salad, fruit
  Ambrosia, 24
  Tropical Breeze, 25
  Tropical Layered, 27
  Waldorf, 26
Salad, Main-Dish, 48–82
  Artichoke Rice, 77
  Boundary Waters, 80
  Caesar, with Grilled Chicken, 53
  Chicken Lagoon, 60
  Chicken Tarragon, 63
  Chicken, Walnut, and Raisin, 62
  Club Chicken, with Hot Bacon Dressing, 64
  Curried Chicken, 66

Grilled Chicken, with Walnut Dressing, 59; *illus.*, 58
Honey Mustard Chicken, 61
Mandarin, 56; *illus.*, 46
Marco Polo, 79; *illus.*, 78
Maurice, 82; *illus.*, 83
Morocco, 68; *illus.*, 69
Oriental Chicken Pasta, 67
Oriental Chicken, with Sesame Dressing, 54
Oriental Turkey, 76
Seafood Louie, 50; *illus.*, 51
Shrimp and Crab Seafood, 48
Smoked Turkey, with Jarlsberg Cheese, 74
Spinach, Supreme with Hot Bacon Dressing, 81
Strawberry Chicken, 52
Turkey Almond, 72
Turkey Citrus, 71; *illus.*, 22
Turkey De Lite, 75
Turkey Twist, 73
Twisted Tuna Pasta, 49
Wild Rice and Turkey, with Raspberry Dressing, 70

Sandwich
Epicurean, The, 113
Field's Special, 111
Frisco, The, 114
Smoked Turkey and Avocado, with Chutney Mayonnaise, 112

Sauce
Brown, 121
Sweet and Sour, 136

Sausage, Italian, and Sage Cream Sauce, Penne with, 124

Seafood. *See also* Name of seafood
Louie, 50; *illus.*, 51
Salad, Crab and Shrimp, 48
Slaw, 33

Short Ribs, Braised, 118

Shrimp
and Artichoke Pasta, 91
and Crab Seafood Salad, 48
and Feta, Mostaccioli with, 93
and Garlic Pasta, 94; *illus.*, 95
with Fennel, Stir-Fry, 87
with Pasta, Spicy, 92

Side Dishes, 130–46

Slaw. *See* Salad

Smoked Salmon and Caviar, Fettuccine with, 89; *illus.*, 88

Smoked Turkey and Avocado Sandwich with Chutney Mayonnaise, 112

Soufflé
Lemon, 168
River Room, 126

Soup, 2–21
Asparagus Soup, Cream of, 13
Black Bean, 9
Cheese, Canadian, 21
Chicken and Cheese, 20; *illus.*, x
Clam Chowder, Manhattan, 11
Clam Chowder, New England, 18; *illus.*, x
Lobster Bisque, 19
Mushroom, Fresh, Cream of, 14
Spanish National, 10
Spinach, Cream of, with Bacon, 17
Squash, Acorn, Roasted, 16
Tomato, Zesty, 7
Tortilla, 8
Wild Rice, Boundary Waters, 12; *illus.*, x
Zucchini and Almond, Cream of, 15

Soup, chilled
Asparagus, Cream of, 13
Cantaloupe, 3
Gazpacho, 6
Peach-Plum-Cranberry, 4
Strawberry, Chilled, 2
Vichyssoise, 5

Southern Pecan Pie, 181

Spaghetti
Marco Polo Salad, 79; *illus.*, 78

Spicy Shrimp with Pasta, 92
Torte à la Andrew, 143
Spanish National Soup, 10
Spinach
Rice Salad, 40
Salad Supreme with Hot Bacon Dressing, 81
Soup, Cream of, with Bacon, 17
Squash Soup, Roasted Acorn, 16
Stir-Fry
Ginger Beef, 117
Shrimp with Fennel, 87
Strawberry
Chicken Salad, 52
Muffins, 161
Soup, Chilled, 2
Sweet and Sour Sauce, 136

Tarragon Chicken Salad, 63
Tomato, Soup, Zesty, 7
Torte à la Andrew, 143
Tortilla Soup, 8
Tropical
Breeze Salad, 25
Layered Salad, 27
Tuna
Grilled with Curry Vinaigrette, 86
Pasta, Twisted, Salad, 49
Turkey
Almond Salad, 72
Citrus Salad, 71; *illus.*, 22
De Lite, 75
Epicurean, The (sandwich), 113
Field's Special (sandwich), 111
Frisco, The (sandwich), 114
Maurice Salad, 82; *illus.*, 83
Salad with Jarlsberg Cheese, Smoked, 74
Smoked, and Avocado Sandwich with Chutney Mayonnaise, 112
Twist, 73
and Wild Rice Salad with Raspberry Dressing, 70

Veal
Geschnetzeltes, 120
Salonika, 119
Veggie and Lemon Pasta Mix, 142
Vichyssoise, 5

Waldorf Salad, 26
Wild Rice
Boundary Waters Salad, 80
Boundary Waters Soup, 12; *illus.*, x
Pilaf, 139
and Turkey Salad with Raspberry Dressing, 70
Wontons, Fried, 137

Yakitori, 106
Yankee Pot Roast, 115

Zucchini, and Almond Soup, Cream of, 15

Ordering Frango Chocolates

Frango Chocolates are made from special time-honored formulations of pure chocolate and the finest ingredients. The rich chocolate centers are poured by hand from copper kettles onto marble tables. After cooling and cutting, each luscious piece is enrobed in chocolate and carefully hand packed. Over the years, the Frango family has grown to include nine tantalizing flavors . . . Mint, Almond, Coffee, Toffee Crunch, Rum, Chocolate Crisp, Raspberry, Peanut Butter, and Caramel.

Frango Chocolates can be ordered by calling our Dayton's/ Marshall Field's/Hudson's toll-free mail-order telephone number: (800) 292-2450.